with love
from
Brother & Shirley

1996.

HEAR OUR PRAYER

For Ruth & Don —
Merry Christmas!
I hope this book serves
you as a source of joy,
inspiration and spiritual
sustenance.

Faithfully,

HEAR OUR PRAYER

Resources for Worship and Devotions

Glen E. Rainsley

United Church Press
CLEVELAND, OHIO

United Church Press, Cleveland, Ohio 44115

Printed in the United States of America on acid-free paper

01 00 99 98 97 96   5 4 3 2 1

Library of Congress Cataloging-in-Publication Data
Rainsley, Glen E.
    Hear our prayer : resources for worship and devotions / Glen
E. Rainsley.
        p.   cm.
    Includes index.
    ISBN 0-8298-1145-1 (alk. paper)
    1. Prayers. 2. Worship programs. I. Title.
BV250.R34 1966
264'.13–dc20   96-28739
                                                            CIP

CONTENTS

ACKNOWLEDGMENTS

My thanks

To PERSONS who used my first book, wrote letters of appreciation, and offered helpful comments and suggestions.

To MELINDA AND CANDACE AND GLORIA, valued colleagues and friends who helped me become a more able minister and who urged me along the path toward producing this book.

To GERDA AND JOE, who have shared with me much of life and faith.

To MY WIFE, SUSAN, whose organizational abilities complemented my chaotically creative style of writing, whose comments always merited heeding, whose word-processing skills proved invaluable to this technologically impaired word-producer.

To MY DAUGHTER, ABBY, who contributed constant good cheer and ample encouragement . . . and who may turn out to be the family's best writer.

INTRODUCTION

WORSHIP AND WRITING are central to my life, so it follows follows that I enjoy creating liturgical materials for congregational use. Five years ago, when presented with the opportunity to produce a book of such pieces, I responded with great glee and with a ready pen. The result (*Words of Worship*, Pilgrim Press, 1991) satisfied a number of personal and pastoral longings: to write a book, to share with others an approach to worship, and to provide usable and easily accessible resources for worship planners.

I had envisioned the resources being helpful to persons entrusted with the privilege of leading worship. And indeed, much of the feedback I received indicated that clergy and laity were using the materials for Sunday worship, regional meetings, family events, fellowship and Bible study gatherings, and occasional services of church-related groups. I had hoped that some readers would find the book helpful in the context of personal devotions, but I was surprised by the number of people for whom this was the book's primary use. For these persons, the book assumed the role of a reference work, a means of finding prayers that would complement and enhance all the other hard work of spiritual development.

Although it has been great fun to see church bulletins from around the country containing materials excerpted or adapted from *Words of Worship*, I have been especially touched by comments and correspondence from those who found the book a source of support and guidance on their personal journeys of faith. As one who exults in the connective, communal, congregational character of Christian worship, I am no advocate of individual spiritual isolationism. We need one another if we are to make progress in faithfulness. And what pleases me immensely is the recognition by many that liturgical forms which comprise the structure of our public worship also relate to private devotional practices. Our life together and our life alone have a spiritual unity.

As I thought about this book, I took into consideration the insightful and much appreciated responses of those who had read the first one. In maintaining the same general format and thematic access, I am keeping what folks seemed to find most helpful. And in intent, my basic goals remain those of providing a resource for worship leaders, inspiring creative approaches to liturgy, and encouraging a poetic prayerfulness. Readers' comments, however, have prompted me to pay greater attention to the ways liturgical materials can become part of personal devotional practices. It is with that potential use in mind that I write the remainder of this introduction and the brief sectional lead-ins.

LIVING AS A WORSHIP EXPERIENCE

One of the consistent messages of Jesus' teaching was that faith has an all-inclusive character. Jesus resisted the attempts of those who wanted to codify it with rules and regulations, challenged those who sought to exempt portions of their lives from faith's influence, and proclaimed the presence of God in all situations. And in the parables, Jesus used examples from everyday life to identify the ways we can recognize God's activity in the midst of the ordinary.

When we take Jesus' teachings to heart, we find ourselves pushed to approach living as a worship experience. If our lives are wholly God's, all the moments and situations within them have holy implications. If our lives are wholly God's, worship must be vocational (our ongoing work as persons of faith) rather than vacational (apart from regular activities). Adopting this approach challenges us to look at our world in an entirely new way. Our vision sharpens. In relationships, we see the opportunity to put a face on the love of God. In events, we sense the upbuilding or impeding of God's reign. In surroundings, we discern symbols that indicate the way God dwells with us.

Developing an understanding of living as a worship experience requires devoted attention and steadfast intention. The process is both demanding and effortless. Sometimes we may wince at what we perceive, for when understanding dawns, it can be as jarring as the first light of morning to eyes that have been closed in sleep. At other times, we may rejoice at what God reveals, for a surprising new understanding can evoke gratitude as we find ourselves able to focus on what had been hazy. A worshipful outlook on life affects us in a wide variety of ways, but always it causes an erasing of the boundaries between the secular and the sacred. Our goal is to be able to identify the transcendent within the temporal, the mysterious within the mundane. The women who reported the resurrection met the Christ outside an empty tomb; we can meet Christ inside a factory or a nursing home. The apostle Paul met the Christ on a public road; we can meet Christ at a laundromat or a fast-food restaurant. Any time. Any place.

Uses of This Book

The ways in which this book can be used by persons charged with planning and leading worship are quite apparent. Its other uses are less obvious, however, so I want to note a few of the uses I envisioned in putting the resources together. These are my hopes.

1. I hope this book inspires the writing of worship resources. Many users of my first book adapted pieces I had written to fit their own needs and contexts; others produced entirely original material in response to reading portions of *Words of Worship*. I am delighted with both uses. Leaders and congregants alike benefit from reflection on the purposes of worship and from engagement in liturgical creativity. The writing process, struggle that it often is, nonetheless remains a reliable means of clarifying what we believe. In matters of faith, progress comes when we find ourselves dissatisfied with saying, "I sort of know what I think (or feel), but I just can't put it into words." That negative sense of discontentment can become a powerful and positive motivator. The task of putting into words our thoughts and feelings about God has the grand effect of making our faith more accessible to us, more available to share with others. Yet it is emphatically a labor-intensive task.

When I casually mentioned to colleagues that I sometimes devoted hours of effort to writing a call to worship or a benediction, a fellow pastor responded, "Are you crazy? What are your priorities?" The first question I chose not to debate. The second question prompted a defense of my decision to put all the energy necessary into crafting words of worship that are meaningful and memorable. After all, worship grounds us as people of faith, shapes us into the body of Christ, equips us for strenuous service in the world. Worship demands our best. No leaden liturgies. No trendiness without substance. No dull or incomprehensible language. Earlier this century, the poet Ezra Pound spent two years working a two-line poem, "In a Station of the Metro," into final form. That example represents an extreme, of course, but everyone involved in corporate worship and personal devotions can take a lesson from Pound's poetic persistence. Though God knows our thoughts and feelings while they are yet silent within us, we honor God with the attempt to express ourselves as honestly and beautifully as possible in any worship context. The materials in this book are simply my attempts at such expression. They serve well to the extent that they encourage others toward approaching worship with a joyful, creative attentiveness.

2. I hope this book takes on, for some readers, the quality of a book of hours. Devotional works that go by this designation present prayers and readings for each hour of the day. At best, their contents are pertinent to the customary activities of readers and may be specific to such things as rising, working, relating to others, pursuing leisure, being alone, resting. The Hebrew Scriptures, whenever they speak of the concept of chosen people, emphasize the steadfastness of God's love through all time and circumstances. The New Testament, as witness to the impact of incarnation and resurrection and presence of the Spirit, reminds us that God is with us always. An awareness of God's involvement in every aspect of our lives grows through our study of scripture. And that awareness begins to transform and enlarge our faith as we carry it with us into our home life, our business relations, our community activities, our hearing of world news. Although most of us do not pause hourly for devotional exercise, we can set aside times for prayers and reflections that connect with the issues we confront daily. The themes used to tag each resource in this book help make these connections.

3. I hope this book leads people to engage in dialogue and to practice solitude. These may seem like contradictory or mutually exclusive aims. Not so. The life of Jesus provides us with a splendid example of what I call the "theology of balance." When Jesus was with people, he listened intently, enjoyed the give and take of conversation, expressed himself with a clarity of willing spiritual self-revelation. When he wanted to be alone, he withdrew from the clamor of crowds to the quiet of the hills or other places apart. In the area of faith development, Jesus' pattern merits our adherence.

We advance in faith by taking advantage of beneficial contacts with our sisters and brothers. A few years ago, a parishioner defined for me why such contacts are important. She said, "The more I talk with folks at church, the more they challenge me, understand me, invite me to voice what I believe, and care for me. They don't allow me to get lazy about my faith. . . . I love it."

Paradoxically, we also advance in faith by retreating. Few of us have the luxury of being able to remove ourselves to a classic retreat spot (Iona or a monastery, for example), but some of us have the opportunity to attend short-term events or renewal-center programs, and all of us have the need to pause for spiritual sustenance. I recently read a worship bulletin that contained a wonderful misprint. The benedictory line read: "May the pace of God be with you." Finding that the pace and peace of God overlap considerably may be one of the most serendipitous discoveries of a faith journey.

The materials in this book are meant to be shared. Ideally, they will draw people together in conversations about matters of faith. The materials are in this book are meant for solitary devotional use. Ideally, they will nourish those who pause to experience the pace and peace of Christ.

4. I hope this book brings plenty of correspondence and conversation. I love getting mail and I enjoy discussing worship with anyone who finds it a topic of interest. The comments, criticisms, and feedback that people shared with me following the publication of *Words of Worship* have helped shape this volume, contributed to worship workshops I have led, and fueled progress along

my own journey of faith. I would consider it a gift to hear from readers and users of this book. For the foreseeable future, I am, by the grace of God, serving the First Congregational Church of Camden, 55 Elm Street, Camden, Maine 04843.

5. Finally, I hope this book becomes yours—a dog-eared friend, a trusted companion, a source of inspiration and joy.

STRUCTURE OF THE BOOK

There are seven genres of worship resources included in this book:

1. calls to worship

2. opening prayers/prayers of confession

3. words of assurance

4. pastoral prayers

5. prayers of dedication

6. introductions to silent prayer

7. benedictions

The book's arrangement permits ready access to a wealth of worship resources. Following the sectional lead-ins introducing each genre, the materials are identified by theme and arranged according to the liturgical year. A user can discover suitable resources by browsing through a section or by consulting the index for specific themes. For example, someone desiring to find a prayer of confession for Lent or a benediction appropriate for common time may simply thumb through the sections designated for these genres. If the quest is for a call to worship related to childlike faith or an opening prayer connected with service or mission, the index will refer to the specific page containing the needed resource. Having dual access routes both encourages perusing and enables precision.

The seven genres included do not cover every worship need, but they do represent familiar core components of many services.

The thematic index is clearly not exhaustive, but it serves as an easy-to-use general guide. I heartily recommend that users add to the index as an increasing use of the resources suggests new thematic connections.

Enjoy using this book. If it contributes to deeper experiences of worship and bolder expressions of faith, God is well served.

CALLS TO WORSHIP

CALLS TO WORSHIP

TELEPHONE TECHNOLOGY has progressed at a rapid rate over the past decade. As a consequence, it can be argued that we are more easily in contact with one another. Some of the changes truly seem to be advances. Audio quality and speed of connections have improved dramatically, and we benefit from the mobility and miniaturization of telephone hardware. We find conference calls and global connections helpful in many circumstances.

Other aspects of telephone technology, however, raise questions worth pondering. The feature known as call waiting comes to mind. Since I cannot really carry on two phone conversations at once, is call waiting designed to help callers or to enhance my sense of self-importance? Are we to believe that people would suffer irreparable damage to their self-esteem if confronted with a busy signal?

And how about the ability to put people on hold? If "Hold, please" are the first two words to greet me, why should I believe there is any personal commitment to get back to me? And who decided I wanted to listen to lousy music while I wait?

Then there is automated dialing. Here is a philosophical question for you: If my answering machine fields the recorded message sent by an automatic-dialing system, has any human communication taken place?

One of the grand features of communication with God is that it has a personal, constant-access, no-pager-necessary quality. Worship, in its many forms, is probably the finest example of a reliable and open communication system. In worship, we speak with God. God speaks with us. We speak with one another. In the setting of public worship, the call at the beginning of the service functions as an invitation to congregants to be both transmitters and receivers, to be communicants in the most inclusive sense of that word.

In congregational gatherings, a clergyperson or lay leader usually offers the call to worship. During the course of our daily lives, however, there are other calls to worship, countless numbers of them, that get issued from another source. When a child shares an insight or an elder imparts wisdom, we are receiving calls to worship. When a fellow commuter becomes a friend or a long-time relationship remains flourishing, we are receiving calls to worship. When the smell of fresh bread reaches us or the sight of a sunrise awes us, we are receiving calls to worship. When a person in need relies on us or a partner on the pilgrimage of faith encourages us along, we are receiving calls to worship.

If we were equipped with the most advanced ecclesiastical technology, its caller ID feature would show us immediately that all those calls have a common point of origin: God calls us to worship every moment of our lives. Whereas incessant phone calls can be annoying, God's courteous persistence is simply amazing. And our most faithful response is that of living in a prayerful, worshipful manner of open communication with God.

Leader: We season our celebration of Advent with bright colors,
People: Colors that touch and teach us as spiritual reminders during this time of preparation.
Leader: The royal purple of candles, stoles, and pulpit hangings
People: Reminds us to be steadfast in repentance, to be forthright in acceptance of Christ's presence in our lives.

Leader:	The evergreen of wreaths, sprays, and Christmas trees
People:	Reminds us to be thankful for our everlasting God, to be hopeful for continuing growth and renewal of faith.
Leader:	The red of poinsettia plants and holly berries
People:	Reminds us to be attentive as God kindles our commitment, to be receptive as the Spirit energizes our actions.
All:	We worship the God who, through the coming of Christ, colors our lives with love.

Advent

▩ Colors, liturgical

Preparation

Centuries ago, a seed of hope for humanity nestled into a tiny crevice of time and place: a time when the promised messiah seemed an eternity away; a place called Bethlehem, a drab town from which nothing good was expected. That seed was vulnerable to the violence of the day, yet by the grace of God it took root in this world and flowered forth as the great and beautiful life of the One we call our Savior.

(This spoken call is intended to be followed by a call in song, "Lo, How a Rose E'er Blooming.")

Advent

▩ Incarnation

Hope

On this first Sunday of Advent, look with gladness toward the season ahead. And throughout these days, keep faith with the coming Christ.

Reject any seasonal pace that allows for no genuine peace.

Refrain from gift-giving that meets obligations but inspires no joy.

Resist any holiday preparations that feel more like compulsions than celebrations.

God provides us this time of Advent to reflect upon the ways of peace, to give thanks for a gift that brings joy to the world, and to celebrate the coming of the One whose love binds together all people. With gratitude to God, we come to worship this morning.

Welcome.

Advent
Preparation
Faithful living

The world is filled with persons for whom peace is a stranger:

> Those imprisoned in cells and those confined by
>   invisible chains of guilt;
> Those without homes and those for whom home is
>   no haven;
> Those affected by the random terror of the streets
>   and those victimized by the organized violence of
>   war;
> Those made refugees by external aggressions and
>   those who find no refuge from internal conflict;
> Those poor in the material necessities of life and
>   those poverty-stricken in spirit.

There is One who can deliver peace to all, though it arrives bearing many names—freedom, forgiveness, justice, mercy, sufficiency, salvation. With keen anticipation and fullness of hope, we look toward the coming Builder of Peace, and we gather in worship to wait and to watch and to welcome together.

Advent
▨ Justice
Peace

Leader:	O come, O come, Emmanuel,
People:	To the empty-handed and the heavy-hearted, to the despairing and the despised.
Leader:	Enter this world,
People:	Giving love to the lowly and hope to the downcast.
Leader:	Dwell among us, and teach us your ways,
People:	Saving the lost and strengthening the weak.
Leader:	Inhabit us,
People:	That we might cast away fear and live boldly by faith.
All:	With gratitude that you come to be with us, we worship joyfully this day.

Advent
▨ Incarnation
Justice

We are not here this evening because of a lack of room at the inn.

Few of us have come here from watching sheep in the hills.

None of us has journeyed from afar by camel.

And more than likely, we did not hear of this gathering from a heavenly host on high.

Yet here we are in a place we knew would be crowded,

Possessing something close to the shepherds' curiosity and joy,

Responding to the light of Christ that lures us and gives us hope,

Hearing somewhere in our hearts ageless echoes of angel voices.

We come as people of Christmas, giving glory to the God who wills peace on earth, the God who comes to be with us. Welcome.

Christmas Eve
Faith, attraction of
Joy

Leader: This night is one of profound mystery.
People: A night for unusual sounds and sights in the heavens.
Leader: This night is one of wonderful clarity,
People: A night for the blessed event of our Savior's birth into this world.
Leader: This night is one of far-reaching complexity,
People: A night for strangers crowding into a stable and for kings starting upon a journey.
Leader: This night is one of touching simplicity,
People: A night for receiving a gift and for cradling God's love in our hearts.
All: We gather to worship on this best of all nights!

Christmas Eve
Wonder
Love, inclusiveness of God's

Once in Bethlehem,
>A tiny voice sounded an infant cry.
>Small hands clutched at manger hay.
>Tired eyes closed to the stable's dimness.
>A fragile life lighted upon the world.

We rejoice this day in the Bethlehem birth, the coming of Jesus our Christ, for as he grew,
>His voice gained the strength of wisdom.
>His hands reached out to all humankind.
>His eyes pierced to the heart of truth.
>His life conveyed a boundless love.

Through him we know that God is with us. Welcome to worship, and glory be to God!

Christmas Day

Love, inclusiveness of God's

Jesus, humanity of

The end of the year is a traditional time for formulating hopes for the future. Hopes come in a variety of forms—in dreams that picture a preferred future, in pulses of creativity that build tomorrow rather than just await it, in spiritual insights that point out passages to the possible. We see hope in children's eyes, feel hope in loving deeds, shape hope in surveying the world around us. In the body of Christ called the church, hopes are encouraged and nurtured and brought to fruition.

For the next few moments, think about one hope you have for the coming year. Then write it on the index card you will find in the pew rack. Later in the service, when we receive the offering, place the card in the plate as it passes. Let your hope be a prayerfully offered gift to the God whose grace works to make hope happen.

Christmastide

Hope

Future

Leader:	We gather this day to praise the God of years calendared into history and moments yet to form the future,
People:	To worship the God of individuals striving for understanding and groups struggling for freedom,
Leader:	To hear the God of prayer's silent voice and scripture's enduring wisdom,
People:	To serve the God of enabling Spirit and faith-in-action.
All:	We gather this day to love our God of all time and all people, of every word and every deed.

New Year
God, presence of ▣
Praise

   The Magi made the most glamourous journey—with the stellar guidance system; the expensive gifts; the intrigues brought on by Herod's insecurity and instability; the dream-borne warning; the infant Jesus, God's child held in a mother's arms. We hear of that journey in scripture and in song, and we celebrate it rightly as a glorious model of faithful response.

   Yet other journeys merit our attention as well. All of us have made journeys of faith that brought us nearer to Christ—when we chose to follow a glimmer of goodness or a ray of hope, when we made an arduous trek from unawareness to belief, when we dared stand against the powers-that-be in service to the Creator of all being, when we discovered the presence of God in an unexpected place or time. This Epiphany Sunday, in hearing once more of the Magi's journey, recall with thankfulness your own journeys as we worship the Christ of star and stable and growing faith.

Epiphany
Faith, journey of ▣
Perceptiveness, spiritual

We come in a variety of shapes and sizes, in a range of ages and states of health.

We come as long-time members and as brand new attenders, as singles and partners, as families and friends.

We come from many religious backgrounds and ethnic origins, from tiny towns and huge cities, from happy homes and turbulent upbringings.

We come with openly expressed needs and hidden hopes, with skills used daily in our work and talents yet to be discovered, with abundant doubts and with firm fervent faith.

We come together. We come to worship. We come to be the living body of Christ, the promising people of God. Welcome.

Community
▩ Church, inclusiveness of
Worship

We move in faith with the freedom of a skater moving upon the ice. Sometimes we glide along effortlessly and smoothly; other times, we stumble because of a flawed surface or our own awkwardness. Sometimes what we intend to do is translated precisely into action; other times, we fall into a heap of poorly executed plans. Sometimes we do well on our own; other times, we need the comforting stability of companionship.

In coming together for worship, we seek to know better the God who helps us remain on our feet in rough times, the God who bids us enjoy the beauty of moving in faith, the God who teaches us to bear ourselves gracefully through all our days. Welcome.

Faithful living
▩ God, need for
Seasons (winter)

It's a strange phenomenon, this coming together for worship. We're really an odd mixture of persons, a hodgepodge of humanity, a potpourri of people. The polite word for us is "diverse."

We're young and old.

We're male and female.

Some of us prefer folk music to rock, others classical to jazz. And vice versa.

Some of us possess many things, others few.

There are Democrats, Republicans, Independents—who knows, perhaps a stray Whig or Tory.

There are social butterflies and solitary folk.

We're sports fans and ballet buffs.

We're joggers and sedentary types.

And here we all are together. We've congregated. It's amazing.

Perhaps the reason we're all here for worship is this: despite all our differences and variety, we have in common a longing to find a way in life and to be found by a powerful, loving God who seeks us and who desires our faith and praise.

Diversity
Church
God, longing for

In baby days of high-chair trays, finger foods, and plastic bibs—we come to the table.

In childhood years of developing tastes, culinary experimentation, and enduring the good stuff to get to the dessert—we come to the table.

In teenage times of fast-food fixes, appetites beyond belief, and dining out with dates—we come to the table.

In adult days of family gatherings, important business lunches, in-flight snack platters, and commuters' hasty bites—we come to the table.

In later years of mealtime meetings with friends, low-cholesterol diets, and solitary suppers—we come to the table.

In every age of life, in order to remember our Savior, to share the warm bonds of faith, and to strengthen our spirits for service in the world—we come to the table. All who hunger and thirst for the fare of our faith, welcome to worship.

Communion
❖ Faith, development of
Common things

All sorts of persons came into the presence of Jesus:

Lepers, accustomed to keeping their distance from others, approached him with the knowledge that—to him—they were not outcasts. He healed them of disease and liberated them from loneliness.

Despised tax collectors kept company with him. They discovered what had been missing in their lives, the companionship that people had withdrawn from them.

A variety of misfits, undesirables, rejects, and sinners sought him out. They thronged to him, longing for the feeling that someone could genuinely accept them as the creations of God and the heirs of God's grace they were.

Children, much to the dismay of decorum-conscious adults, flocked to Jesus' side. He embraced them, for in their spontaneous trust, the children embraced the truth of God's realm.

We who gather for worship are persons somehow drawn to Christ. And we come as so many before have come, in need of healing and companionship, seeking gracious acceptance and welcoming love. With these, the reign of God reveals itself in our midst. Welcome.

Faith, family of
❖ God, reign of
Love, inclusiveness of God's

Leader:	We come from a week of hollow loneliness and incomparable companionship, strained relations and graceful understandings.
People:	We gather this morning to reach out in good will toward our sisters and brothers in Christ.
Leader:	We come from a week of sharp heartaches and gentle joys, wrenching stress and healing recreation.
People:	We gather this morning to seek rest and renewal for our spirits.
Leader:	We come from a week of straying commitment and positive purpose, blurred focus and keen insight.
People:	We gather this morning to center ourselves in worship, confessing Jesus Christ as our Savior.
All:	To the Creator God who draws us together, we offer heartfelt thanks and praise.

Praise
Gratitude
God, longing for

Leader:	For the order of creation that reveals itself through cycles of time and patterns of nature,
People:	We offer our thanks and praise to God.
Leader:	For the order of human relationships that reveals itself in balances of togetherness and solitude, reliability and surprise,
People:	We offer our thanks and praise to God.
Leader:	For the order of our faith that reveals itself in ministries of Word and sacrament, social deed and individual reflection,
People:	We offer our thanks and praise to God.

All: We gather to worship, seeking the order of
discipleship and the freedom of Christ's way.

> Praise
> ◈ Order
> God, as Creator

This morning we step into the season of Lent as persons
embarking on a pilgrimage. May we have the wisdom to equip
ourselves well—with a sturdy trust in the forgiveness and
lovingkindness of our Creator, with a firm reliance upon the
guidance of Christ, and with a complete confidence in the Holy
Spirit to provide sustenance throughout the journey. May we
move forward with the alertness demanded by discipleship,
with the humility and honesty of maturing faith. May we walk
well together, extending to one another comfort,
encouragement, and good company. Welcome.

> Ash Wednesday
> ◈ Faith, journey of
> Discipleship

We take notice of the following purple things:
> The purple folds of distant misted hills,
> Spring's first flowers, clouded sundown skies,
> The purple richness of royal garb,
> The purple glint of dew-drenched grapes.
During Lent, we celebrate with purple a season when our
spirits are colored by reflection and repentance.
     In the weeks ahead, may we acclaim this world's Creator,
confess the reign of Christ in our lives, and drink in the Spirit's
power. Welcome to worship.

> Lent
> ◈ Colors, liturgical
> Repentance

There is no real chill to unkindness or neglect.
There is no real weight to the problems we carry about.
There is no real dimness to a closed mind or an
empty heart.
Yet when our faith is real and true—
Love for others warms us with faith's fire,
God's guidance and forgiveness remove burdensome weights
from our spirits,
An inspired wisdom illuminates our outlook,
And a desire to do what is right and just releases us
to action.
In gathering to worship, we affirm our faith as a real power
in our lives. Welcome.

Lent
Faithful living
God, power of

Imagine ahead to warming days when strenuous work or
hard play or bold heat of spring and summer sun cause great
thirsts—
Thirsts that lighten the head and set muscles aquiver,
Thirsts that drain us of energy and leave us limp,
Tongue-thickening and guzzle-grabbing thirsts,
Thirsts that claim all our attention, thirsts that must be met.
Great thirsts also affect our spirits, especially when we feel
the heat of searing stress or blazing anger, demanding decisions
or exhausting sorrows.
Imagine now a well dug deep into the bedrock of
faithfulness, filled with water cool and clean and refreshing. In
worship we draw forth that water. In service to others, we taste
it. In looking ahead, we trust in its supply. This day we gather to
give thanks to the God who provides all who thirst with Christ,
the water of life. Welcome.

Lent
Thirst, spiritual
God, trust in

Leader:	We come here this day to wait upon one another,
People:	Sharing the presence of God in the passing of bread and cup.
Leader:	We receive here this day sustaining gifts from a ministering Savior, a table-host Christ,
People:	Who pours out forgiveness and fills us with love.
Leader:	We leave here this day to serve in the world,
People:	As bearers of good news to persons who hunger and thirst in body and spirit.

Lent
Mission/service
Communion

Leader:	How tempting this morning to lounge about the house or to linger over breakfast.
People:	We come to worship with awakened faith and hungering spirit.
Leader:	How tempting it was this morning to continue perusing the news or chuckling through the comics.
People:	We come to worship seeking enjoyment of God's good news and participation in the community of the church.
Leader:	How tempting to be elsewhere.
People:	How grand to be here!
All:	We come to worship the God of all creation, the Christ who brings salvation, the Spirit of truth and liberation.

Lent
Temptation
Worship

A setting sun leaves behind its colorful statement of farewell, itself a promise of tomorrow's reappearance. A scurrying animal leaves behind both its scent and its track, records of its presence and activity. A growing plant leaves behind the seeds or bulbs that bear new life, assurances of continuity in the future. A departing friend leaves behind memories rich with caring and sharing, connections that cannot be broken.

Today, as we gather for worship, we celebrate what Jesus Christ left behind—a table and a sacramental meal. These are signs that speak to our faith. They serve as promises of our Savior's reappearance, records of divine presence and activity in human history, assurances of continuity for the body of believers, reminders of a holy and unbreakable connection with our Creator.

To worship we come, offering thanks and praise to God.

Lent
Communion ▨
God, sensing

Leader: Manger-born and a craftsman by trade, teller of
            stories and friend to children, he turns toward
            Jerusalem.
Children: Hosanna!
Leader: Teacher and living Word, healer of the infirm and
            hope-bearer to the lowly, he approaches the Holy
            City.
Women: Blessed be the One who comes in the name of
            God!

Leader:	Interpreter of tradition and guide to new ways, preacher by parable and revealer of truth, he rides into Jerusalem.
Men:	Hosanna in the highest!
Leader:	Gentle conqueror and servant sovereign, powerful prophet and lover of God and neighbor, Jesus enters into our lives.
All:	Hosanna! Blessed be the One who comes in the name of God! Hosanna in the highest!

Palm Sunday
▣ Jesus, humanity of
Praise

If we knew that Jesus was journeying on his way here instead of moving toward Jerusalem, what sort of road signs might we put before him?

Considering our oftentimes dim understanding and dull response to God's Word, a sign alerting Jesus to such SLOW CHILDREN might be appropriate.

And noting that the ways of our culture clash and collide with the will of God, a sign designating this a DANGEROUS INTERSECTION might serve to warn the approaching Christ.

The notion of Jesus coming here shakes us as well as excites us. Perhaps we're not quite ready, not quite able to handle Christ's presence, so we put up DETOUR signs. And maybe we can't accept that there are many ways Christ can choose to enter us, so we try to mark the route we want by posting a ONE WAY sign—our way.

Christ is always poised to come into our lives. May our gathering to worship serve as a friendly town's sign by the roadside saying, WELCOME TO THIS PLACE! WELCOME INTO OUR MIDST!

Palm Sunday
▣ Signs
Jesus, impact of

Leader:	Because the story must be shared,
People:	We gather together on this day of resurrection.
Leader:	Because Christ lives,
People:	We offer our thanks on this day of resurrection.
Leader:	Because the love of God knows no limits,
People:	We voice our praise on this day of resurrection.
Leader:	Because joy fills our spirits.
People:	We celebrate this day of resurrection.
All:	By the grace and power of God, Christ is risen, and we are set free to live for our Savior.

Easter
Resurrection
Freedom

No matter how often the dawn heralds day's beginning with sounds and light, we always welcome the sense of newness that morning gives.

And no matter how many times we hear the Easter story proclaimed in song and gospel, we always welcome the assurance of newness that Christ's resurrection gives.

By our Creator's design, the predictable transition from night to dawn is a matter of course.

Through our Creator's power, the wondrous transition from death to life is a matter of grace.

Thanks be to God! Christ is risen!

Easter (Sunrise)
God, power of
Newness

Leader:	This day we look upon the cross that held no hope and heralded no future, and we see it as the sign of power and promise.
People:	Christ is risen! Our Savior lives!
Leader:	This day cannot contain our joy, for the tomb could not contain the One who is our Savior.
People:	Christ is risen! Our Savior lives!
Leader:	This day the loud hosannas of welcome become alleluias of praise to a living Savior.
People:	Christ is risen!
All:	Christ is risen indeed!

Easter
Cross
Praise

Leader:	Thursday's Last Supper had been a time of sorrowful goodbye. Now it comes to new life as a sacrament of joy.
People:	Christ is risen!
Leader:	Grim Friday had left the followers of Jesus bereft. Now it comes to new life as a wondrously Good Friday.
People:	Christ is risen!
Leader:	The cross had borne the man of Nazareth into defeat and death. Now it comes to new life as sign and symbol of God's triumph.
People:	Christ is risen!
Leader:	The tomb had sealed its mouth and swallowed up the promise. Now it comes to new life, and its silent emptiness proclaims the fullness of God's love.
People:	Christ is risen! Christ is greatly to be praised!

Easter
Cross
New life

Most of the candy is gone now, although there may still be a bit of chocolate rabbit's ear or tail, or a couple of jelly beans down beneath the strands of fake grass.

The holiday ham has disappeared in a week of sandwiches, and maybe its scraps have gone to the family dog or cat, or to a trash-scavenging raccoon.

No one is looking for eggs anymore, but perhaps a forgotten one—chocolate or hard-boiled—that was left beneath a radiator is beginning to make itself remembered.

All these parts of Easter's excitement have gone by, but the cross is still with us, still empty, and Christ is still alive. And that is ample and abundant reason to gather together for worship of our God. Welcome.

Eastertide
Cross
Resurrection

We come from the labors of factory and field, the business of office tasks, the chores of home tending, the efforts of classroom and workshop.

We have used our hands to create and assemble; now we clasp them in prayer or extend them in a reach of friendship.

We have focused our minds on projects and plans; now we attune them to the mind of God.

We have exerted ourselves to make sales; now we receive as a free gift the forgiveness purchased by God.

We have provided services of all kinds; now, as persons seeking to serve in the Savior's name, we await the Spirit's direction.

Welcome to God's sacred workplace, this worship place, this home for the faith family.

Faith, family of
Work
Grace

With electron microscopes, we probe the mysteries and intricacies of life within a cell.

With magnifying glasses, we detect small flaws in objects and enlarge tiny print so it can be read.

With binoculars, we discern the flick of feathers amidst branches or the flash of winged flight across the sky.

With the orbiting Hubble telescope, we peer into the infinity of space to examine its features.

From the minutest particle of matter to the outermost reaches of time, the creation pulses with the presence of our living God.

With the imagination of open minds and the worship of loving hearts, we look upon the greatness of God and offer our thanks and praise.

Welcome.

Perceptiveness, spiritual
God, greatness of
Gratitude

Leader:	When going out to dinner, it makes a difference to our emotional state whether the evening's companion is a critical new boss or a comfortable old friend.
People:	When listening to a concert, it makes a difference to our eardrums whether the performers are a chamber ensemble or a heavy metal band.
Leader:	When hanging a door, it makes a difference to our preparation whether that door will secure a bank vault or enclose the broom closet of a wooden dollhouse.
People:	When riding a bicycle on a steep mountain trail, it makes a difference to our leg muscles whether we are riding uphill or downhill.
All:	When living in this world, it makes a difference to our spirits whether we serve the one true God or some impostor power. This day as we gather for worship, we witness to our faith in God.

Choice
Common things
Faith, call to

In God's creation, age is a sign of grace. It is evocative of bold images and feelings.

The ancient oak, tallest in the wood, stands proudly with branches reaching above surrounding trees—a sense of dignity presides.

The mountains—"old as the hills"—surge up with quiet strength to assure no bland horizon. A sense of reverence arises from them.

The sea, life's cradle, tosses its tides in affirmation of its own aliveness. A sense of constancy asserts itself.

The sun, old Sol, creates skyscapes each day to celebrate renewal and rest. A sense of energy flows forth.

Perhaps these portions of the creation remind us that the God of old is yet with us today. Our Maker who calls us children endures from age to age. So let us worship God, and may a sense of gratitude fill our time together.

> God, steadfastness of
> Age
> Creation

Leader: We gather to worship the God who crafted the whole of creation, yet who can be neither contained by its expanse nor fully described by its beauty and majesty.

People: We gather to worship the God who gave birth to our entire human family, who brought us into being, in all our diversity, as bearers of the divine image.

Leader: We gather to worship the God who inhabits every second through all eternity, who animates us with the breath of Spirit and inspires us with the call to serve in Christ's name.

People: We gather to worship the God who bids us build a healthy global home filled with justice and peace, who equips us with a capacity for mercy and compassion.

All: We gather this day as God's people, brothers and sisters to one another, proclaimers of good news in every time and place.

> God, as Creator
> World
> Brotherhood/Sisterhood

There are so many calls for our attention:

The compelling cries of infants and the urgent expressions
of a friend in difficulty,
The flashing signs of a coach and the terse directives of a
boss at work,
The lingering echoes of our upbringing and the hard demands
of present decision,
The quiet beckonings of a simpler life and the insistent
urgings of a consumer culture,
The soothing sounds of nature and the recurrent pleas of
people in need.

Today, our presence for worship proclaims that we have
heard the call of God to gather together, to work as partners in
faith, to discern through dialogue with one another how best to
respond to that which claims and clamors for our attention. May
we listen for the good Word of God with spirits intent and alert.
Welcome to worship.

Faith, attraction of
God, Word of
Choice

Leader:	It was the power of God that let the enslaved Hebrews go forth from pharaoh's bondage into the perilous freedom of the wilderness.
People:	All praise be unto God!
Leader:	It was the power of God that inspired rejoicing among the citizens of Jerusalem as they responded to the invitation, "Let us go to the house of God!"
People:	All honor be unto God!
Leader:	It was the power of God that let Jesus go from death's entombment to a life redemptive for all humanity.

| People: | All thanks be unto God! |
| All: | As we worship this day, we offer praise and honor and thanks to God. |

God, power of
Praise
Gratitude

Leader:	When I was a child, I used to look for God
People:	In dim closets or up in the sky or in sunlit places among the shadows.
Leader:	When I was a child, I used to listen for God
People:	In the thunder or the wind or the silence beneath the covers on a cold winter's night.
Leader:	When I was a child, I used to reach for God
People:	With questions or prayers or the imaginings of my spirit.
All:	Today we come as children and adults to be together as the church family. We come to worship the God we look and listen and reach for all our lives.

Faith, childlike
Community
God, sensing

Leader: To "give a hand" is to express our gratitude or satisfaction, as through appreciative applause. To "give a hand" is to offer ourselves in helpfulness or concern, as through deeds of kindness.

People: This day we gather as people who rejoice that our lives are in the hands of God, as people who give thanks that that our hands can accomplish God's work in the world.

Leader: Whether our hands are gnarled or nimble, thick-fingered or dainty, weathered and leathered or smooth and tender,

People: We extend them in prayer to God.

Leader: Whether our hands are clumsy or graceful, injured or unscathed, strong and mature, or child-sized and growing,

People: We extend them in service to our neighbors.

All: In good faith, we reach out to give a hand so that the love of God might be proclaimed, so that the will of God might be done on earth.

Hands
Mission/service 🔲
God, will of

Leader: We come to God as people crawling or caning our way along, people striding confidently or stepping hesitantly through life.

People: And always God welcomes us and draws us closer.

Leader: We come to God as people attempting or attaining success in communication, people making sounds without words or putting thought and feeling into language.

People: And always God hears us and invites us to come near in the conversation of prayer.

Leader:	We come to God as people discovering or defining our faith, people exploring tugs toward commitment or developing a system of belief.
People:	And always God encourages us and reaches out to us.
All:	We worship this day our gracious God who accepts us, listens to us, and embraces us with steadfast love.

Faith, journey of
Grace
God, love of

Today is Pentecost, a day of remembering and celebrating afresh the coming of the Spirit. At first glance, it might apear that we are especially receptive to the Spirit's arrival and activity because the notion of "spirit" is familiar to us.

We try to build up a "team spirit" among both workers and players.

We cultivate a "public spirit" in our citizens.

We cherish "spirited" conversation and wonder at the ways of those we call "free spirits."

But none of these things defines us as "spiritual" in the Pentecost sense, for where is the Spirit called Holy making itself known among us?

We who worship this morning gather as the church, born on Pentecost, child of the Holy Spirit. May we open ourselves to being touched and transformed. Welcome.

Pentecost
Spirit
Church

I once heard a child who was just awakening give voice to the best of ways to greet the day: "Good morning, God. I love you." For this or any worship service, those words of welcome and adoration serve as a simple statement of praise.

Because today is Pentecost, a time when we are especially aware of the many languages spoken throughout the world, I'd like to ask how many of you can say, "Good morning, God. I love you," in a language other than English.

(Ask each volunteer to say the phrase and name the language.)

There are many ways to say, "Good morning, God. I love you." And it's important for us to remember when we say it that we are connected to millions of other folks. Let's try something here. When I raise my hand, I want everyone to say, "Good morning God. I love you," in one of the languages just named. Then, when I lower my hand, all together say the words printed in the bulletin, "We are one in the Spirit, we are one in God."

(Do exercise by raising your hand, lowering your hand, and concluding with, "We are one in the Spirit, we are one in God.") So may it be.

Pentecost
Community 🔷
Praise

Leader:	We come together this day for worship;
People:	We gather as the children of God's family.
Leader:	We seek to form a relationship with God that has the quality of childhood friendships,
People:	A relationship open and buoyant, one unencumbered by ulterior motives and restrictive demands.
Leader:	We seek to nurture a curiosity about God that bears the marks of childlike wonder,
People:	A curiosity bold and intense, one generated by a Spirited desire to know and to grow.

Leader:	We seek to build a faith in God that extends the beliefs of the child within us,
People:	A faith trusting and courageous, a faith developed through personal ponderings and dialogue with others.
All:	With joy and gratitude, we join together in worship.

> Faith, childlike
> Wonder
> Growth

The rainstorms of the past week can serve to remind us of our Creator's presence and power.

The Spirit of God comes upon us as the rain, as baptismal waters that feed our hopes, that cause the seeds of faith to germinate within, that enable beliefs to blossom into action.

The rains that fall to earth gather in streams that vein mountainsides with living waters, in rivers that carve a course through the land, in oceans that swell and surge and break into spray upon the shore. The Spirit is like these waters— life-giving, course-setting, and soul-refreshing. With thanks for the presence of God's Spirit in our midst, we gather this day for worship.

> Spirit
> Baptism
> Seasons (spring)

Leader:	God's covenant with creation was sealed with a rainbow. For its signature colors we give our thanks.
People:	For the red of ladybug wings and apple skins,
Leader:	For the orange of sunfish bellies and tangerine pulp,
People:	For the yellow of egg yolk and pollen dust,
Leader:	For the green of broccoli stalks and mountain cover,
People:	For the blue of cloudless sky and rolling sea,
Leader:	For the indigo of bunting feather and mollusk shell,
People:	For the violet of iris petal and ripened plum,
All:	We give a world of thanks as we come together for worship.

Covenant
Colors (liturgical)
Creation

Through every age and in every place, the Christ in whose name we gather calls disciples with a simple invitation, words of challenge: "Come follow me."

And where is it that we go with Christ?

Christ leads us among enemies and strangers, causing us to regard all persons as potential friends.

Christ leads us into uncharted places of spiritual wilderness where the Word and will of God are the only reliable guides.

Christ leads us to lose ourselves just so we might be found, just so grace might become real.

And Christ leads us toward the apparent dead-end of a cross to reveal a highway to new life.

We gather to worship the Christ who leads. May we gain the wisdom and courage to follow. Welcome.

Discipleship
Faith, development of
Mission/service

We come to worship with faces deep-scored with years, smooth with youth, faces animated by our feelings, covered by our public masks, faces expectant and wary, faces intent and inquisitive—all faces somehow turned toward the face of God.

We come to worship with hands strengthened by long use, hands altered by injury, hands calloused from labors, hands softened into tenderness, hands stiff or supple, hands expressive or stoic—all hands somehow reaching toward the hand of God.

In this time together, our faith comes to life in the turning and reaching toward God. Welcome to worship.

> Diversity
> Faces
> Hands

Have you ever noticed all the different kinds of clouds that summertime brings? There is something alluring and wondrous about clouds that captures our attention. Perhaps they serve as a way the Spirit speaks through creation to tell us of our God.

Those swift, thin, wispy clouds of an almost-clear day are the Spirit's shorthand announcement of God's grace-fullness and quick-moving love.

The bold rolling storm clouds with dusky-dark and violet underbellies remind us that ours is a God of power and might.

The floating fleece clouds that graze slowly across the sky's blue fields tell us of God's peace.

And the clouds of sunset, rosy orange and golden hearted, proclaim the glory of God.

This is the season of clouds, and perhaps the God who led the people of Israel with cloud by day speaks to us through them yet.

The grandeur of God is all about us. We come to worship the Creator of all. Welcome.

> God, as Creator
> Clouds
> Seasons (summer)

We have known the pain of finding a favorite toy broken by constant use and have winced when a broken bone was the result of hard play.

We have endured the breakup of relationships and behaved in ways that pushed parents or partners to near-breakdowns.

We have felt the twinge of breaking away from the place of our upbringing and have savored the joy of breakthroughs in the growth of spirit or intellect.

We have experienced broken bonds of friendship and have faced interruptions in our planned career course.

We have recognized, in moments of clear and honest reflection, that someday there will be a break with life itself.

This day we gather to worship the God whose love makes us whole amid brokenness and gives us hope in all circumstances. Welcome to worship.

Brokenness
Hope
Wholeness

Leader:	We gather to affirm the warmth of our faith, giving thanks . . .
People:	For the connectedness that forms whenever Christ convenes us, for the caring that marks us as a church community.
Leader:	We gather to receive the nourishment of our faith, giving thanks . . .
People:	For the prayers that strengthen our spirits, for the energizing power that Word and sacrament release within us.
Leader:	We gather to celebrate the texture of our faith, giving thanks . . .

| People: | For the human diversity that characterizes us as a family, for the multiple ministries that call us into God's service. |
| All: | We give heartfelt thanks for a faith to savor and to share. |

Gratitude
⬚ Worship
Affirmation

There are plenty of things that can weigh upon us, get us down, overload our capacity to function ably and gladly.

These things come from outside us (a boss's imposed deadline for completing a project) and also from inside (a nagging compulsion to succeed or prevail at any cost).

These things are sometimes expected (the demands of raising children or caring for aging parents) and often unexpected (the loss of income or a sudden health problem).

These things may be lingering (ongoing debts and unresolved feelings) or they may be short-term (a tough task that gets addressed and accomplished).

All of these things are among the burdens we bear and share as human beings, the burdens that wisdom and worship bid us entrust to God's power. Welcome.

Burdens
⬚ God, power of
Wisdom

The signs will be all around: the boxy yellow buses on the streets; the stray jackets or hats dropped on the ground in the heat of recess competition; the soggy fragments of notes to parents that show up in the washing machine; the peculiar sound of silence in some homes. School soon begins or has already begun, and children are heading back to classrooms again.

It is helpful at this time of year to realize that the church as a whole is something of a classroom, too. Going to church implies that we are students, students of the Spirit who have a lifelong curriculum:

We learn the mathematics of love that shows us how the more we give away the more we have remaining.

We expand our language skills by talking with God, listening to one another, and discovering that the Word conveys intricate meanings and miraculous power.

We explore the science of the natural things God has made, appreciating the wonders upon wonders that have evolved from the Creator's mind.

We find in our social studies that all people have value in God's sight, and that interdependence is the way of humanity.

And we feel through music and art a creative union with the imagination of God.

May we learn well the ways of faith in our time of worship and throughout the course of life.

Education
Faith, inclusiveness of
Discipleship

Leader: To viewers of *Sesame Street*, to builders of block
            castles, to keepers of stuffed-animal zoos, to users
            of thick crayons—to you Jesus says:
People: "Come. Follow me."

Leader:	To students eager and reluctant, to skateboarders and owners of head-hugging radios, to starving victims of homework hungries—to you Jesus says:
People:	"Come. Follow me."
Leader:	To workers wearing T-shirts or tailored suits; to laborers in home and office, schoolroom and boardroom, factory and field; to apprentices and pros—to you Jesus says:
People:	"Come. Follow me."
Leader:	To retirees who wear the years well, to stay-at-homers and far-and-wide travelers, to rememberers of long ago—to you Jesus says:
People:	"Come. Follow me."
All:	As followers of Jesus Christ, as disciples, we come together this day for worship.

Discipleship
Community
Diversity

Today is Sunday, and Sunday is part of the weekend. It's a time of worship between the week that's ended and the week that's beginning. In a way, our worship is like a punctuation mark in time.

Worship is like a question mark that lets us ask about God and express our wonder, our curiosity. It lets us ask God to increase our faithfulness.

Worship is like a period that allows us to pray, to learn, to reflect upon the way we live. It allows us to pause for a while with God.

Worship is like an exclamation mark that encourages us to be glad and enthusiastic in serving God. It encourages us to remember the joys of faithfulness.

Welcome to worship. It is good to be together with God and with one another.

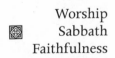

Worship
Sabbath
Faithfulness

Leader:	With sunrise, new light comes to a waking world.
People:	For this time of worship, we gather as people with dawning understandings, with spirits stretching, and reaching toward the bright and beckoning wisdom of God.
Leader:	With midday, full sun falls upon us.
People:	For this time of worship, we gather as people with daylight understandings, with spirits illumined by experience and developed by exposure to the faith of others.
Leader:	With sunset, subsiding light signals a period of rest and renewal.
People:	For this time of worship, we gather as people with evening understandings, with spirits comforted by insights already gained and challenged by hopes and dreams yet to form.
All:	Thanks be to God for this time of worship.

Faith, development of
Time
Worship

Leader:	We gather to hear about the story of our faith,
People:	About God's mighty acts, about the brave deeds of prophets and heroes, about the noble work of persons who live out a commitment to Christ.
Leader:	We seek to immerse ourselves in the story of our faith,
People:	By striving to find our role within it, by interpreting it anew as it touches our spirits and circumstances, by allowing it to change us.
Leader:	We hope to be ongoing participants in the story of our faith,

People: As translators of love into action, as creators of justice and peace, as characters who confront life with a true sense of devotion.

All: In worshiping God, in listening to one another, we celebrate the story of our faith.

> Faith, story of
> ▦ Transformation
> Mission/service

These things we meet face-to-face on a regular basis:

• a sometimes-frightening image in the morning mirror
• familiar expressions of friends and relations
• ongoing concerns and unsolved problems
• needs of neighbors near and far
• human failings and limitations
• opportunities for service and for expansion of our faith
• revelations of our Creator's grace and power

May our worship together give us the spiritual discernment to see, in all these things, in every life experience, the loving face of God. Welcome.

> God, face of
> ▦ Common things
> Faithful living

Leader:	We gather today as the people of God, as a community of Christ's followers.
People:	We gather to share Word and sacrament, to discern the ways of faithful service.
Leader:	Where in the world shall we serve our God?
People:	At home and school and business place—in this community and throughout every land.
Leader:	How in the world shall we serve our God?
People:	By working toward justice where there is oppression and openness where there is prejudice—by offering comfort where there is pain and love where there is hatred.
Leader:	Why in the world shall we serve our God?
People:	Because the Spirit beckons us, because Jesus calls us to enact our faith.
All:	We give thanks that we are in the world, in service to God.

World Communion Sunday
Mission/service
Justice

Change is one of life's constants. At worst, it's something we resist and contend with; at best, it's a sign of God's grace and an opportunity for growth.

There are time changes—setting back clocks, varying the tempo and pace of life.

There are temperament changes—shifting attitudes, movements toward new understandings and feelings.

There are nature's seasonal changes—frosting windshields, scurrying squirrels and chipmunks doing their winter shopping among the fallen leaves.

There are our own personal changes—developing identity, acknowledgment that we are somewhat different today from who we were a week ago or a year ago, or many decades ago.

This morning we gather to worship the steadfast God who accompanies and guides us through all the changes of our lives. Welcome.

Reformation Sunday
Change
God, steadfastness of

There are many firsts that we enjoy and celebrate: the arrival of the day's first light, the first falling snow in winter or budding blossoms in spring, the first friends found in a new home town. Through these things we develop an appreciation for changes and nature and community.

There are many firsts that we note and remember: a child's first word, a first kiss given and received with romantic intent, a first job that converted work to pay. Through these things we discover the promise in conversation and love and labor.

This morning we gather to worship the Creator of all things. May we offer the first stirrings of praise in our spirits, the first portion of our resources, the first affections of our hearts. Welcome.

Stewardship
God, allegiance to
Priorities

Most of the time we carry one or more of the following items with us:

- cash, credit cards, checkbook
- cash in quantity enough to give us a sense of buying power or a feeling of security that we will not be caught short
- credit cards that allow us to act with immediacy while deferring consequences to the future
- a checkbook filled with pieces of paper that receive value only as we place our name upon them

All of the time we carry with us presences of the living God:

- love in quantity enough to rely upon as source of power and security in every circumstance
- hope that urges us to act now out of trust in the God who grants us our future
- faith built upon steadfast contact with the Holy One whose values we cherish and whose image we bear

Funds we find useful. God's presence we find vital. So it is that we gather this morning to worship our Creator, Sustainer, and Comforter. Welcome.

Stewardship
God, presence of
Values

We have much for which to be thankful. There are moments in our lives that grace us with a sense of awe or insight or privilege or contact:

We come upon a stand of leafless trees communing in the lunar light with a gentle clack of branches.

We discover within ourselves a priceless spiritual gift hitherto unwrapped, unused, unknown.

We connect with someone who can talk with us faith to faith about our concerns and joys.

We recognize in the eyes of a homeless old man or a South African child or a Haitian mother God's call to loving action.

These gracious moments in our lives, as well as our lives themselves, are gifts from God. This morning we gather in worship to extend our thanks to the Creator of all.

Thanksgiving
Grace
Common things

OPENING PRAYERS

OPENING PRAYERS

THE FACT THAT MOST worship services have some sort of opening prayer is hardly surprising. We expect to pray when we go to church. We are entirely open to the notion that prayer will be part of our worship activity.

One of the good news features of our faith is that if we adopt a worshipful approach to our whole life, the openings and opportunities for prayer are constant and countless. This may sound overwhelming, even burdensome, but in truth, there is no greater liberation than that which is born of a prayer-based lifestyle. Because prayerfulness requires an attitude of love and passionate caring, we develop through praying a nonjudgmental sensitivity toward others and a perspective on issues and situations that is undistorted by selfishness. Also, because prayerfulness acknowledges our reliance upon God, our praying releases us from any compulsion to concoct solutions and so frees us to act with genuine grace.

Prayerfulness is the opposite of passivity. It is the starting-point for activism. A thoughtful parishioner once described her experience of prayer in this way: "I used to think praying was a cop-out, a pious excuse for doing nothing. Then I started praying about one specific concern. I wasn't sure what to do, and I wanted God to provide me with a course of action. Well, God did not tell me what to do. But through prayer, I developed a new attitude toward the problem, and with that new attitude in place, I gained a sense of clarity about how to proceed. This was not what I had expected. I wanted to change a situation; God first changed me. I wanted an answer; God gave a new way of seeing. I wanted an action plan with neat goals and objectives; God activated my ability to use the gifts I possess in a responsively loving manner. That, I discovered, is what prayer does—it activates."

The openings for prayer are as numerous as the events in life. Read the newspaper or listen to a friend's troubles—respond with intercessory prayer. Take on a new obligation or make a difficult promise—offer a prayer for strength. Hear God's voice in a child's laughter or wonder at the wonders of nature—construct a prayer of adoration. Savor a cup of coffee or do a good job at work— rejoice with a prayer of thanksgiving. Ignore an injustice or speak untruthfully about another person—employ a prayer of repentance. Prayer takes shape as we pursue the routines and standard tasks of daily life.

Consider the following closing thoughts on the subject of opening ourselves to God and adopting a worshipful approach to life. . . . First, if confession is truly our desire to be open before God and open to receiving an activating power, then it must be our primary form of prayer. Second, whenever we own up to the sins and faults and failings that weigh upon us, we find that we are able to take ourselves more lightly, to move with more spritely steps along the pilgrimage of faith. Confession serves as the starting place for an open relationship with God, as the point of origin for all other forms of prayer. It merits a high-priority presence in public worship and personal devotions.

Loving God, we shall soon begin the unpacking process, for we have moved into a new season of the church year. During the days of Advent, we unpack beloved scripture stories, well-loved carols, remembrances of holidays past, decorations for halls and walls and mantels. Help us to do so with attentiveness and joy.

Mighty God, we feel alive in spirit, for we are keenly anticipating events ahead. During the days of Advent, we anticipate familiar festive smells from the kitchen, parcels and letters in the mail, reenactments of long-standing traditions, arrivals of guests. Help us to do so with appreciation and contentment.

Gracious God, we reach out toward you and toward our neighbors, for we recognize the abundant opportunities for giving. During the days of Advent, we give holiday hugs to many, support to persons in need, serious thought to our Christian calling, focused attention to the wonder of your love. Help us to do so with reverence and imagination.

We long to celebrate the Christ-child's birth, and we desire to keep close company with you in our weeks of preparation. Amen.

Advent
▨ Preparation
Celebration

Loving God, we offer our praise and thanks for your radiant presence in our lives.

Although we have a tendency to avoid full exposure to your brightness, for we prefer to linger in the shadows of our doubts, we also recognize that only your light can cause our spirits to grow and to flourish. Grant us the wisdom to live completely and openly in your presence.

Because a variety of things impair our vision—among them, prejudice and selfishness and resentment—we often have a dim perception of your will for us. We grope about for a way of faith in a world of many paths. Clear our vision, we pray, that our actions and choices might truly serve to reflect your light.

In spite of a deep desire to be faithful, we regularly seek after other sources of illumination. And we are disappointed when they do not help us to see more clearly. Help us to turn toward you with consistency and trust.

We offer our prayer in the name of Jesus Christ, whose birth signifies the dawning of new light upon the earth. Amen.

Advent
▨ Faith, vision of
Selfishness

Great and gracious God, during the remaining days of Advent and throughout the Christmas season, fill us with the kind of wonder that enables a true appreciation of your gifts. Help us acknowledge with our praise your artistry as Creator of this world, your wisdom as Teacher and Guide, your compassion as comforting Healer, your justness as Sovereign over every portion of our lives, your love as Parent of the One who came to share our humanity and to reveal your will.

Magnify our faithfulness, O God. Grant us the strength to set aside the false standards that measure greatness in terms of accumulation and influence, power and empire-building. Turn us toward the example of Jesus, for he showed that genuine greatness derives from generosity and cooperation, empowerment of others and dedication to the building of your realm.

Come into the midst of us and dwell within us. We greet the Christ-child with gratitude and hope. Amen.

Advent
God, names of
Faithful living

Mighty God, anticipation grows within us as hope waiting to be born. Tend our days, we pray, so faith will flourish and love will prepare a home for the coming Christ.

Grant, O God, that we may find some peace and quiet throughout this Advent season. Teach us to be reflective about the account of Jesus' birth, to hear the scripture story not as a time-worn tale, but rather as timeless good news. Inspire us to pray for the world you created and for the human family you bless with your presence. Move us toward personal and corporate commitment to walk in the way of peace.

Grant, O God, that we practice peace in action beyond this Advent season. Enable us to be reflectors of your light as our faith brightens with every opportunity to serve. Strengthen us to love with the gentle power required by justice and released by grace. Help us, as we journey in faith, to join with Christ in constructing the way of peace.

We give glory to the Bringer of Peace. Amen.

Advent
Peace
Brotherhood/Sisterhood

O God, in the closing days of this Advent season, grant a spiritual alertness that will prepare us well to receive the coming of our Savior.

As we decorate a Christmas tree, may the placing of every ornament be an act of celebration, and may the inhaling of the evergreens' scent be a reminder of your Spirit's freshness.

As we sing carols with others, may the glad blending of voices be a model of our cooperative companionship in Christ.

As we look at creche figures and watch pageant actors, may the wondrous story of Jesus' birth nestle into open and hopeful hearts.

As we light four candles in the Advent wreath, may the flames serve to signal your power and to assure us of your presence through the full circle of our lives.

We offer this prayer in the name of Bethlehem's bright child. Amen.

Advent
Preparation
Common things

O God of Word and promise, God of wondrous new birth, we gather to worship in the name of One who is Word made flesh, who is the promise kept, who is born to us a Savior. Hear our prayer.

During this time of year, God, we find ourselves making brisk dashes to parties, flurries of trips to malls, customary holiday visits to relatives. Amid all our travels, our goings here and there, grant us the wisdom to see that when the spirit of Christmas is alive within us, we are necessarily on a journey of faith.

So much lies before us as we travel on.

The light of hope is on our horizon signifying your presence in the world, even in unexpected Bethlehem-like places. Draw us into the light.

The small stable, such an ordinary place, surprises us with the greatness it contains. Enable us to discover other pathways into the holiness of the commonplace.

The angelic proclamation of Jesus' birth, news too good to be untrue, hovers before us like a carol frozen in the winter air. Encourage us to pursue the follow-up story of our Christ's life and teaching.

Beckoning and sustaining God, we acknowledge with thankfulness your coming among us, and we trust in your guiding accompaniment on the journey of faith.

We offer this prayer in Jesus' name. Amen.

Christmas
Faith, journey of
Common things

God of Christmas, we give you thanks this day for a love alive, an earth-dwelling love announced long ago by angelic voices sounding on high and by an infant's mangered cradle cry. We give you thanks for a surprising and true story told in flesh and blood, told through the centuries as sustaining good news.

Help us, we pray, to move from receptive thankfulness to an active extension of the Christmas message.

Keep us ready to welcome your presence with a Mary-like openness of faith, and a Joseph-like trust, for we need both of these traits to overcome our hesitations at doing your will.

Grant us a headlong, shepherd-like eagerness to be with you, a strong desire to participate in the great things that you do, and an abiding wonder that you call us to bear witness to your Child, this world's Redeemer.

Enable us to grow with the Bethlehem child, expanding our love for you in ways that make every deed of every day the expression of our faith. Mold our spirits to be as Jesus'— durable and daring, generous and joyful, creative and caring.

In Christ's name we pray. Amen.

Christmas
Inclusiveness
Worship

O God, ever since you appeared to the Magi in a Bethlehem stable, you have continued to reveal yourself in surprising ways, and you have promised your steadfast presence in our midst. Help us to see you as clearly as travelers of old saw the guiding star.

Amid the clashes and reconciliations of nations, the cries and laughters of a living creation, enable us to discern your presence in all the world.

Amid the cooperations and competitions of our jobs, the stresses and satisfactions of producing goods or services, enable us to discern your presence in the workplace.

Amid the accomplishments and procrastinations of daily life, the disciplines and doubts of faith, enable us to discern your presence in our spirits.

We seek you with open hearts and reach toward you with the desire to serve. In the name of Jesus Christ, we pray. Amen.

Epiphany
Work
God, presence of

Loving God, we give thanks for your support and sustenance already given, and we look with hopeful spirits toward your steadfast presence in our future. Help us to become ever-wiser men and women as we journey in faith together. Hear in this prayer our deep desire to move ahead as people renewed and guided.

Forgive our wanderings, those times when we choose to go our own way while ignoring the course we discern as your will.

Forgive our inattention to the needs of those who walk the earth with us, those beset with burdens of injustice, deprivation, and despair.

Forgive our unwillingness to acknowledge that you are our sole provider, that your Spirit is the power source for all true progress.

Forgive our haste in matters of faith, our reluctance to linger with the Bringer of Peace.

Gracious God, though we stray off course, yet we seek Christ in order to follow you. Help us on our way. In Jesus' name. Amen.

Christmastide
Faith, journey of
Forgiveness

Gracious God, you have given vitality to the church by letting your Spirit flow through its words and work and worship. You have made us a servant people, a holy household, a family of faith. You have called us to be active as the body of Christ in this world.

Keep us fit as a body of persons in service to others. Grant us the will to become peacemakers and reconcilers, the endurance to exercise compassion, the wisdom to practice the Christly cross-training of sacrificial love.

Keep us healthy as a body of persons striving toward holy living. Teach us to nourish ourselves with your Word, to incorporate into every deed the teachings of Jesus, to convey a spirit of healing in all circumstances.

Keep us strong as a body of persons desiring to develop in faith. Enable us to build a firm sense of community, to discover the power of gentleness and love, to strengthen one another through offerings of support in times of need.

Help us, we pray, truly to be your church. In the name of Jesus Christ. Amen.

Church, as body
Spiritual training
Mission/service

Loving God, we offer our prayer as people moving in faith, peole striving to discern your will and your way, people seeking to form a church responsive to the guiding of your Spirit.

Inspire us to be a grateful church, one that comes to a true appreciation of your abundant grace.

Enable us to be a resourceful church, one that uses to your glory the abilities of all within it.

Strengthen us to be a faithful church, one well aware that forgiveness requires change of heart, that peace takes the effort of building, and that righteousness leads in the direction of justice.

Encourage us to be a hopeful church, one bold in the belief that a vision of your realm calls us to action within the world.

Through the life of your church, you connect those of us in this place with people throughout the earth. We offer our thanks and our praise. In Jesus' name. Amen.

Church
Faith, components of ◈
Spirit

Gracious and compassionate God, who alone can guide us into a life that finds the true freedom of faithfulness, we offer this prayer as the honest expression of searching spirits.

We confess that, by attitudes and actions, we have impeded the progress of some persons who struggle to move toward freedom. We have allowed ourselves to benefit from injustices to others. We have kept multitudes of your children shackled with chains of prejudice or stereotype. We have applauded our own decency while refraining from deep spiritual self-appraisal.

We confess that, by habit or neglect, we have often chosen to use our freedom unwisely. We have succumbed to doing things that harm our health or adversely affect the well-being of our spirits. We have sacrificed growth in relationships by shackling ourselves to rigid patterns of behavior. We have settled into the prison of faith undared.

Forgive us and set us free indeed. In the name of the liberating Christ. Amen.

Freedom
Prejudice
Irresponsibility

Merciful God, we speak this prayer as a grace said before the meal that nourishes our faith. We voice our gratitude for what you set upon the table.

> Thanks be to you, O God,
> for the cup of blessing that signifies both the
> compassionate sacrifice of Christ and the
> assurance of freeing forgiveness,
> for the bread of life that unifies us as we
> participate in its breaking and strengthens us as
> we share in its serving.

As persons who hunger and thirst for a close relationship with you and for loving companionship with other persons, we ask that you help us acknowledge those things we must ourselves bring to the table.

> We offer to you, O God,
> our receptive spirits and expanding faith,
> our desire to pour out talents in a manner that
> leads to the fruition of your will on earth,
> our longing to be as a leaven of hope and a flavor
> of joy within the daily bread of world events.

We come to Christ's table to receive your love and power, to give our commitment and praise. In Jesus' name, we pray. Amen.

Communion
Gifts
Grace

Loving God, on this day of annual meeting, we pray that you build us up as a congregation. Structure us for service in Christ's name.

Help us form a firm foundation of belief and action based upon Word and sacrament. May our spirits remain stable when events shake the very ground of our being, when worldly powers threaten to undercut our commitment to justice and righteousness and Christly love.

Permit us to develop, in community with one another, a feeling of sanctuary, a sense that the peace of Christ lives within us and among us. May our spirits recognize this church as a safe haven in turbulent times, a place of caring support and consistent good counsel.

Grant us a program of outreach that stands as a spire against the sky, as a witness to your love amid the needs of the world. May our spirits stretch as we reach to minister to others, as we shape the inspirations of prayer into deeds of mercy and compassion.

Enable us to frame our faith according to your will as you extend to us the Spirit's constructive power. In Jesus' name, we pray. Amen.

Faith, structure of
Sanctuary
Mission/service

O God, we pray this morning that you fill us with your Spirit in a way that fosters a fitting attitude of worship, one rooted in humility and growing in love.

We want to be humble as Jesus was, in a way that lifts up those with whom we have contact, in a way that leads us to practice servanthood with such devotion that your name is exalted through us. Protect us from the arrogant desire to be better than others; enable us, by your grace, to be better to them in sharing, better for them in deed, better with them in understanding. Help us to see that true humility is a trait to be strengthened; grant us the courage and patience that are necessary for humility to develop.

We also seek to be loving as Jesus was, in a way that excludes no one, in a way that brings the reality of your reign to bear on the affairs of this world. Urge us to love boldly, realizing that the cost of love gives it value, the sacrifice of love renews its life, the tenacity of love makes it enduring. Inspire us with an expanding ability to trust in love's power, for that power is unlimited when faith sets it free.

In drawing us together, you provide us with the opportunity to build one another up and to express love. May we do so with a sense of joy and glory, for the sake and in the name of Jesus Christ. Amen.

Humility
Inclusiveness
Jesus, as model

Loving God, we acknowledge to you our need for spiritual order and support. Hear our prayer.

We confess to discouragement at the scattering about of friends and families, at the fragmentation we sense within our world. Connect us with one another, we pray.

We confess to discomfort at the clutter of trends and values our culture displays, at the lack of insight and integrity within its systems. Clear our hearts and minds, we pray.

We confess to distress at the disarray we find when we assess our hopes and intentions, at the mixed messages and multiple allegiances we allow to govern our lives. Align our wills with yours, we pray.

Grant us an acceptance of your guidance, a commitment to heed the direction you offer. In Jesus' name. Amen.

Order
Commitment
General

Loving God, with confidence in your grace and reliance upon your power, we dare to offer our prayerful words of confession. We have not lived the fullness of faith. Forgive us.

We have loved you with less than our entire selves, and we have strained against the notion that need defines neighbor.

We have treated the nourishment of our spirits more as optional than as vital, and we have exercised our devotion inadequately.

We have allowed faith to be tamed by the culture, and we have accepted a domesticated variety lacking in holy wisdom and Christly courage.

We have developed spiritual laryngitis when justice bids us be advocates, and we have used prayer more for complaint than for praise.

We have served faulty ideals or false idols, and we have missed deeds of compassion while doing misdeeds of uncaring.

Forgive us, we pray. And by your love, redirect us. In the name of Jesus Christ. Amen.

Unfaithfulness
Justice
Faith, requirements of

O God, we awaken each day to a world that is habitat for Spirit and humanity, to a world that invites our participation in a complex of holy tasks and relationships, to a world that challenges our faith with both its promise and its pain. Within this world, your presence is prominent, yet we often miss it out of negligence, ignore it out of willful inattention, or dismiss it out of disbelief. Forgive us.

Grant us, we pray, a sharp spiritual vision that permits us truly to see the real world. Encourage us to dwell in such a world:

• a world where the practice of humble service is a valued and noble calling
• a world where commitment to Christ beckons us toward ventures of community and cooperation

• a world where compassion for generations yet to come makes inconceivable our misuse of the earth
• a world where matters of Spirit occupy the place of highest regard

Inspire us to participate in the mission of doing your will on earth so all persons might know the reality of your love. In Jesus' name. Amen.

World
Future
God, love of

Loving God, we give thanks that your world is our home. You have decorated it with canyons and cascades, open oceans and intricate inlets, broad deserts and deep rainforests, mountains and plains. The beauty of our home is wondrous to behold. You have stocked it with plentiful resources of food and water, materials for construction, and areas for recreation. The bounty that surrounds us in our home amazes us. You have filled it with companions of all sorts, furred and feathered, scaled and shelled, species upon species. The blend of inhabitants within our home enriches us.

Forgive us, we pray, for the poor care we give to the home you provide us. We have made alterations that destroy the work of your hands and that weaken the good earth's structure and balance. We have wasted supplies, spoiled our living space, and acted with irresponsibility as tenants of your world. We have consumed without conscience as if our greed had no consequences for our neighbors.

Grant us a renewed appreciation for our home, and charge us with the reverence and responsibility to keep it well. In the name of Jesus Christ, creation's Ruler. Amen.

Earth Day
Environment
God, as Creator

Loving God, we confess freely that all is not well with us. We seek your encouragement and renewal, your forgiveness and grace. We pray for the wounds of our world and ask that you enable the community of faith to wield restorative power.

Help us to heal injuries caused by cutting words and deeds, by the sharp cruelty of neglect or uncaring.

Help us to smooth feelings hurt by unnecessary abrasiveness and rough handling.

Help us to care tenderly for all persons bruised by the brutality of disaster or injustice.

Help us to repair the damage done wherever violence punctures peace or lurks about as the threat of harm.

May the church be a wellspring of hope, the primary source for waters of life. In the name of the Holy One, Jesus Christ. Amen.

Lent
Healing
Violence

Loving God, from the days of old when you formed a group of nomads into a nation, to the present time when you gather us into a worshiping community, you have connected faith with servanthood. Seeking to be faithful to your purpose and your calling, we pray that you enable us to be:

• people who preserve life through our commitment to be the world's peacemakers and the creation's caretakers

• people who observe with prayerful attention the events and relationships that build our human history

• people who reserve judgment and practice understanding when confronted with those who differ from us or disagree with us

• people who serve to spread the good news of our faith in a manner both humble and powerful

Through Jesus Christ, we pray. Amen.

Lent
◈ Servanthood
History

Gracious God, we offer this prayer as people seeking to mature in faithfulness and striving to contribute all we can to building up the community that gathers in Christ's name. Forgive us when our seeking loses its intensity or lacks focus, when our striving gets lethargic or goes in undesirable directions.

Forgive us our unkindnesses. We have allowed our words to be more hurtful than healing and have succumbed to judgmental attitudes.

Forgive us our indifferences. We have constricted our caring by turning away from problems we would rather not see and by extending only a safe and selective form of compassion.

Forgive us our unavailabilities. We have shied away from callings to exercise our talents in your service and have made ourselves spiritually or emotionally inaccessible to others who need us.

Forgive us our insecurities. We have let the doubts of our faith impair the boldness of our actions and have often failed to believe how thoroughly you value and love us.

Relying upon your power to forgive, we pray in honesty and hope. Through Jesus Christ. Amen.

Lent
◈ Faith, laziness in
Irresponsibility

Loving God, we pray that you make the weeks of Lent a time of pilgrimage and a spiritual growing season, and we ask for the wisdom to claim it as a period for slowing our pace and for developing a sense of personal peace. Help us, by your grace, to overcome the temptations that divert us from paying attention to your will, temptations that prevent us from attaining fullness of faith.

When we are tempted to neglect worship, recall us to a deep enjoyment of Word and sacrament.

When we are tempted to become self-centered, remind us that it is you who made us and not we ourselves.

When we are tempted to ignore the health of your creation, renew our understanding of stewardship for the earth.

When we are tempted to value convenience over compassion, restore our capacity to care deeply.

Grant us, during the Lenten season ahead, a discipline and direction that will strengthen and guide our spirits. In the name of Jesus Christ. Amen.

Lent
Temptation
Faithful living

Loving God, in baptism we participate in the life and death and resurrection of Jesus Christ. The sacrament calls us to make a commitment and to affirm our faith. It bonds us to one another through a promise of support. For this visible sign of a vibrant faith, we offer our thanks to you.

And we voice our gratitude for faith itself. Although we are ultimately responsible as individuals for the choices we make, you draw us together in community to learn from brothers and sisters who are, with us, Christ's disciples.

We are grateful for a challenging faith. Although we sometimes ignore its origins, deep within we understand how faithfulness is formed in wilderness places. For the Hebrew people, it was in periods of wandering and exile; for Jesus, it was in times of desert temptation and prayerful trial; for us, it is in moments of need and instances of doubt. Help us maintain a vital faith, resisting any urges to tame or domesticate it, to make it more palatable than powerful.

For a developing faith, we offer our thanks. From early in our lives, you provide us the opportunity to keep company with others, those who will nurture faith and be present in trying times. We grow with your support and by your grace. We pray in Jesus' name. Amen.

Baptism
Wilderness
Faith, development of

Gracious God, we have assembled as followers of Christ, as people who strive to be leaders in the doing of your will. Grant us an affinity for the outpouring quality of our Savior's love and for the servant character Jesus commends to spiritual leaders. Help us to recognize, through study of scripture and attention to experience, that for all persons and all time, Jesus left behind both the poetry of his teachings and the power to shape disciples.

We pray that you energize us with your creative and sustaining Spirit. Enable us to be bearers of hope to the stricken, companions to the lonely, up-builders of the downcast or down-and-out. Through our worship, may we come to deeper understanding of our alliance with Christ and our reliance upon Christ. Inspire us to confront the enthronement of false gods in our lives and in our culture. And give us the courage to practice what our faith calls us to do. In the name of Jesus Christ. Amen.

Lent
Leadership, spiritual
Discipleship

O God, we recognize Jesus' entrance into Jerusalem as an act of faith and courage, for he knew that the power of your love would be challenged by those in power within the city. He knew that the far hills were safer, the cheering crowds were fickle, the enemies were devious and determined. Yet he laid his life on the line, and we are the grateful beneficiaries of his steadfast reliance upon you. Give us the strength to climb out of the safe hills of our lives and enter our own Jerusalems. We acknowledge that our faith promises risk as well as triumph. Place an awareness of this within our hearts as we celebrate the day of palms. We pray in the name of Jesus Christ, who risked his life to give life. Amen.

Palm Sunday
Courage
Faith, risks of

God of love and majesty, we come together this morning as a crowd came together in Jerusalem long ago—welcoming the One we dare to call Sovereign and celebrating the arrival of the One we know as Bearer of Hope. We offer bold words of praise and make solemn commitments to follow.

Forgive us, we pray, for letting our faithfulness disperse as the welcome wears thin, as the way gets difficult, as the week goes on.

Our demand that Jesus meet our own expectations often leads us to pay little attention when the true Christ is revealed to us. Forgive us.

Our selfish goals or narrow hopes prompt us to balk at Jesus' call to lose ourselves gladly in the service of others. Forgive us.

Our flawed understanding of power's true source causes us to withhold commitment and to mistrust Jesus' utter reliance upon you. Forgive us.

Speak to us anew. Refresh our spirits on this day of palms. In the name of Jesus Christ. Amen.

Palm Sunday
Selfishness
Faith, challenges of

Almighty God, we pray on this Palm Sunday that Jesus enter into our lives as he entered into Jerusalem—to words of welcome and praise. May the power of Christ dwell within us. Set our spirits on fire, cause a commotion in our souls, enable us to choose to be with Christ when the cheering stops.

Through the days ahead, open us to insight and change so the week becomes truly holy for every one of us.

Overturn our wrongdoings as Jesus overturned the moneychangers' tables.

Wither our selfishness as Jesus withered the fig tree that bore no fruit.

Expose our failings as the course of events exposed those of betraying Judas, denying Peter, and doubting Thomas.

We begin this week with anticipation, O God, for the old story becomes new again with the receiving of palms.

Surprise us. Focus us. fill us with wonder at a servant Savior, a donkey-rider and washer of feet, One who gave all for us. In Jesus' name, we pray. Amen.

Palm Sunday
Commitment
Faith, surprises of

O God, we come tonight at the invitation of Jesus Christ to share a sacred meal. It is a gracious host indeed who shares not only the bread and wine but also, selflessly, life and being. As we come to the table, we notice a betrayer, a denier, a doubter, and a group that sits in startled silence. Yet all find welcome.

In sharing this time of communion with you, with one another, with persons of faith throughout the earth and throughout the ages, help us to understand that this meal provides us with a taste of your eternal reign. Whet our appetites for service, and nourish us with your presence. In the name of our host, Jesus Christ. Amen.

Maundy Thursday
Communion
God, reign of

O God, at this holy time, we look upon an empty cross and offer thanks for the fullness of meaning it bestows upon our lives. We gather in worship as a joyous resurrection people.

More than a good story emerged from that first Easter day. You wrote into history the enduring good news of your steadfast love, your abundant mercy, your refusal to give in to death-dealing powers.

More than a rock-hewn tomb opened up. You opened wide the possibilities of faithful living by turning despair into exultation, by transforming sacrifice into triumph, and by changing the followers of a crucified carpenter into the disciples of a risen Christ.

More than one life was restored. New life was given to all humanity, for through the victory of Christ, burdens drop away, hatreds cease to bind us, and even the most tenacious sins lose their deadly grip.

More than words of praise are due to you, O God, so we pray with great hope that you will guide us toward service and lead us into all the ways of faithfulness. In Jesus' name. Amen.

Loving and powerful God, Creator of all life, we give thanks that by the exercise of your love you have transformed the world.

You have shown a boundless grace and an unlimited capacity to forgive.

You have released us from bondage to our sins and entombment in our deepest fears.

You have opened the way for establishing justice and peace.

You have declared your absolute unwillingness to abandon us, no matter what we do to put you off.

You have encouraged us to dare the boldest of hopes.

You have, through Christ's resurrection, redeemed and renewed us.

Transform our gratitude into discipleship, our beliefs into enactments of your will and expressions of an enduring Easter faith. We pray with joy in the name of our risen Savior, Jesus Christ. Amen.

O God, we gather to worship this morning because Jesus Christ is alive as our Teacher, Companion, and Savior. Your grace and power transformed death to life. So from the living Christ we learn to carry out a risky, unselfish love; through Christ we experience a surprising and reconciling oneness with others; and toward Christ we express a wholesome, grateful praise.

We confess that sometimes our risen Savior does not occupy the heart of us. We trivialize Christ's teachings or dismiss them as impractical ideals, out of touch with the realities of our world. Sometimes we are less than constant to Christ; we let our concern for Christ slip away if our association causes unpopularity or pain. And sometimes we fail in maintaining an allegiance that places Christ first and foremost; we worship other idols and therefore worship Christ with incomplete devotion. Forgive us. Forgive us and restore us. Make us your resurrection people—eager learners, spirited searchers, bold believers, faithful followers.

In our time together, may the wondrous power of the resurrection touch us deeply. We offer this prayer in the name of the risen Christ. Amen.

Easter
Faith, challenges of
Discipleship

O God, in this time after Easter, help us to understand with all our being that we are a resurrection people. Prevent us from being merely spectators staring at an empty cross or peering into an empty tomb. Rather, charge us to be persons who strive toward receiving the power that used emptiness as a means of revealing fullness of life. How tempting it is, now that Easter is past, to lapse into believing that sin and death again hold sway, that resurrection can be packed away as past event. Forgive us when we succumb to temptation and allow the life and laughter, the hope and happiness of Easter, to be interred within. Grant us the wisdom and the courage to trust in a present power of resurrection that enlivens every day.

Enable us in our worship, in our work, and in our leisure to meet Christ, to realize that our Savior is not someone dead whose day has come and gone, whose work is finished. Help us to acknowledge with our responsive love that Jesus is with us today as our living partner, guide, and companion. And remind us that, in a world where there is yet much good to be done, only a living faith will do.

Hear our prayer, offered in the name of Jesus Christ. Amen.

Eastertide
Resurrection, power of
Jesus, companionship with

Loving God, our walk in faith is less a path of ease than it is a struggle to remain upright. We confess our need for your support graciously offered to those who seek forgiveness.

We trip up in the pursuit of developing faith as we stub our spiritual toes on neglected prayer and casual commitment.

We slip upon the slighting words and thoughts generated by unadmitted prejudice.

We skid into an easy selfishness, one that allows us to defer consideration of how our actions have an impact on others.

We stumble over ethical decisions that pull us toward difficult understandings, that demand genuine changes of heart and practice.

We fall headlong into making unholy choices that harm others by ignoring their plight or contributing to their pain or refusing to hear their truth.

Forgive us, we pray. By your grace, grant us forward-looking faith and stability of spirit. In the name of Jesus Christ. Amen.

Faith, journey of
Choices
Selfishness

O God, we praise you as Creator of everything that exists, as Provider of all that is good and just, as Comforter of those in distress, as Enabler of joy and peace, as Redeemer of humankind.

We petition you in times of thorough despair or compelling crisis, and we profess the belief that an exercise of your power can obliterate evil or hasten healing. We trust in your power and might.

Yet again, our trust is limited. We confess to toppling you from the priority position in our lives, especially when faithfulness contradicts desire or when commitment to Christ becomes a disturber of comfort. We shrink your impact upon our decisions by listening to your Word with selective hearing. We neglect to offer thanks for the grace and bounty that mark so many of our days. And we back away when you beckon us to become instruments of your power as peacemakers, liberators, healers, and bearers of steadfast love.

Almighty God, forgive us. Renew our trust. Embolden our faith. In the great name of Jesus Christ, we pray. Amen.

Trust
God, names of
Unfaithfulness

Loving God, you have bid us be your witnesses in this world. Strengthen us, we pray, for taking on that task and for responding to your call with commitment.

We confess that often our ways of witnessing have been halting or haphazard. Because our spiritual senses suffer from poor development or ongoing neglect, we miss observing even the most emphatic examples of your living presence in our midst—the embrace of sturdy friendship, the honest statement of truth, the needed nudge toward action, the awakening to appreciation of creation, the achievement of a clarity that enables us to believe with wholeness of heart.

Forgive our inadequate testimony to the power of your love within our lives. We have acted as though you were indifferent to our strivings and failings, as though the condition of our spirits mattered little, as though the resurrection never occurred. We have been more dour than daring with our faith, more restrained than venturesome. fill us with your presence in such a way that we come to speak and act with humble conviction.

In the name of Jesus Christ, we pray. Amen.

Witnessing
God, presence of
General

Loving God, you have called us to be your witnesses in the world. Grant us your guidance and sustenance.

As we listen to the Word that beckons us to enact our beliefs, help us to become people of purpose and responsiveness.

As we confront conflicts on levels both individual and international, help us to become people of peace and kindness.

As we sense the need for bold profession of healing good news, help us to become people of power and gentleness.

As we commit ourselves to a course of spiritual growth, help us to become people of prayer and hopefulness.

By your grace, may we witness well to a firm faith in Jesus Christ. Amen.

Eastertide
Witnessing
Discipleship

We give thanks today for this church, and we pray that for years to come its people and its programs will boldly proclaim your love for humankind.

We thank you for the faith of those who formed this congregation, who set a course of ministry that has endured through the years.

We thank you for the fortitude of men and women who have labored in your service through trying times of revolution and civil strife, religious ferment and financial hardship.

We thank you for the compassion of church people, generation upon generation, who have helped to shape this community and to give it a character of caring.

We thank you for the courage of those who have taken up the causes of justice and peace, who have affirmed faith as dynamic and all-embracing.

We thank you for a goodly heritage and a promising future. Relying upon your sure presence and steadfast love, we look back with appreciation and look ahead with hope. In the name of Jesus Christ. Amen.

Church, anniversary
History
Time

Gracious God, help us to see the many ways we can crown Jesus Christ as Sovereign of our lives.

In the prayers spoken in Jesus' name, may we create a crown of words that will identify our needs while honoring Christ as head of the church.

By transforming animosities into friendships, may we shape a crown of love that will produce buds of reconciliation where thorns of hatred once were.

Through every kind and caring deed, may we form a solid crown of service that Christ will place lightly yet securely upon us.

And in all our praise and worship, may we ourselves become as living crowns that display within the world your glory and power. As subjects of Jesus Christ we pray. Amen.

Christ, sovereignty of
🔲 Faithful living
God, reign of

Compassionate and caring God, we find the process of letting go a strain upon our spirits. We acknowledge that what it demands of us is often more than we offer.

We decline to let go of things that poison us—vengeful thoughts, self-righteous judgments, unconfessed guilts, unconfronted prejudices.

We hesitate to let go of things that hinder our personal growth—lingering hurts, hard feelings, unreconciled grievances, unresolved griefs.

We refuse to let go of things that tempt us—enticements away from our values, neglects of our faith co mmitments, rejections of your will, suppressions of our boldest hopes.

Free us toward being able to let go of all that is more harmful than holy. We ask this in Jesus' name. Amen.

Forgiveness
🔲 Freedom
Stubbornness

God our Maker, we are grateful that you created us free and curious persons, inhabitants of this beautiful earth. You have revealed your love for us by giving us both the capacity to make choices and the ability to heed your guidance. We are students in your world, O God, and as we pass through the years, help us to remain eager learners of your ways.

With the Bible as an open book in our hands, may our minds open as well.

With Jesus as teacher and example, may our hearts enlarge in discipleship.

With your Spirit as inspiration, may our wisdom increase.

fill this time of worship with your presence. In the name of Jesus Christ, we pray. Amen.

Education
Choice
Discipleship

Loving God, we give you thanks for this season of the year, a time when the air fills with sounds and wings, when ponds ripple in response to springtime breezes and movements of feeding fish, when the scent of soil reminds us of its fertile warmth, when streams react to sudden showers with quickened pace and flow. In this season, we feel the power of renewal. And we pray that our spirits may fill with this power as you graciously provide it, reveal it, and nurture it within us. Grant us the wisdom to identify Christ as the One who indeed empowers us, not only from one season to another, but for all eternity.

When we are beset by problems that hover about us like gnats, enable us to cope. When we are troubled by pains that seem as persistent as weeds, strengthen us with patience. When we are congested in spirit by sins as potent as pollen, help us to inhale freely your wisdom and grace. Loving and powerful God, renew our lives. In the name of Jesus Christ, we pray. Amen.

Seasons (spring)
Empowerment
Renewal

Loving God, we confess to dealing with your creation in ways that have been irresponsible and irreverent. Our spirits have been polluted by selfishness or by lack of appreciation. We have abused the earth that is your gift to us, and thereby we have offended you. Forgive us and redirect us.

We have worked at cross-purposes with our finest intentions. We care for the immediate environment with attentiveness and concern, and bemoan the atrocities that destroy or despoil ecosystems throughout the earth, yet we have maintained patterns of wastefulness and consumption that pain our planet. We have demanded more than our share of resources, defended our privilege, and kept the damage distant so others can be blamed. Forgive us and redirect us.

Empower us, we pray, to become more able and active stewards of your creation, to regard it as a trust that will bear continuing witness to your glory and that will be the secure habitation of future generations. Make us truly caretakers and help us to live lightly upon the earth.

Seeking your forgiveness and your direction, we pray in Jesus' name. Amen.

Earth Day
Environment
God, as Creator

Caring and compassionate God, we offer a simple morning prayer of petition.

When we feel inundated by a flood of troubles, grant us a buoyancy of spirit.

When we feel perilously submerged beneath our sins and failings, enable us to take hold of your forgiveness so we might emerge to new life.

When we feel that the course of our lives has become misdirected, channel our energy toward the doing of your will.

When we feel that circumstances have eroded our trust in you, restore us to fullness of faith.

We pray with confidence in the name of Jesus Christ. Amen.

God, power of
Water
General

Gracious God, we give you thanks for drawing us together as the church. We confess that sometimes we feel as the early disciples must have felt when Jesus departed from the earth. There are pangs of separation and abandonment, for we are not satisfied with promised power. We wonder how the Spirit will minister to our needs and sustain our faith.

Hold us together, O God. Forgive us when petty irritations or prejudiced views or selfish attitudes cut into the cords of love that bind us. Preserve us from a frayed faith, from the severing ways that rule this world but have no place in your church.

Teach us, O God, of the power released when your people unite in praise and service. When we are bound together, we sense true freedom. When we join our hands, we reach out to others with amplified strength. When we encourage one another in the pursuit of justice and peace, we avoid the brittle boldness of acting alone. When we adhere to the ways of Christ, we cohere as a body of believers.

Enfold us with your Spirit. And as we experience the joys and challenges of life together, keep us in your care. In the name of Jesus Christ. Amen.

Ascension Day
Unity
Church

O God, we gather here to worship, confessing that we are needful of your presence and guidance and support. We yearn for your Spirit to come among us and live within us. And yet our yearnings are tempered by a hesitancy to become more for you than for ourselves, tempered by feelings of uncertainty about our own capacity to lead spiritually centered lives.

We pray that your Spirit be as a wind. Let it be the winds of the Spirit that awaken us with bracing gusts and carry us to new places. Teach us to soar with your winds of change rather than remain grounded by our own foggy understandings and set ways.

We pray that your Spirit be as a fire. Let the flame of the Spirit test us and light our way. Enable us to see that the fire does not consume us but rather kindles us and sets free the energy stored within.

O God, touch us, fill us with your Spirit on this day when the church was born. In the name of Jesus Christ, our model of faith and spirited living. Amen.

Pentecost
Spirit
Change

Gracious God, we pray this morning for a faith that embodies the best of being a child. Let it be alive with a spirit of playfulness, for joy is an able teacher. Allow it moments of renewing serenity akin to those that bless the sleep of dreaming children. Grant to our faith a five-year-old's willingness to ask direct questions and appreciate the mysteries that answers cannot explain. Charge us with the energy of youth as we put our faith into action.

Compassionate God, we ask your forgiveness of childish behaviors that prevent us from fully maturing in spirit. We confess to doing what we know better than to try. We practice individual and collective selfishness that insists on its own way, that balks at the guidance of others, that approaches life with a "me first" attitude. We make a mess of our surroundings through emotional inattention or ethical unconcern.

Shape us as your children. Help us to be bright with the spirit of truth and understanding. In the name of Jesus Christ. Amen.

Faith, childlike
Maturity, spiritual
Selfishness

God of creativity and compassion, justice and peace, you have called us to be people who place faithfulness at the heart of our lives. Yet, however much we strive to let Christ reside at the core of our being, to center our attention on the Spirit's activity, we fall short of full devotion and close ourselves to complete empowerment.

> Forgive us, we pray,
> for coldness of heart that has led us to ignore the
> alienated and reject the misunderstood,
> for weakness of heart that has prevented us from
> befriending our enemies and encouraging the dispirited.

Forgive us
for puny attempts to heal the broken-hearted of
your world,
for significant neglect of glad-hearted praise,
for heartless and hurtful deeds.

Help us to reclaim a healthy and wholehearted faith, alive
with the desire to spread the good news of your love for
humankind. In the name of Jesus Christ. Amen.

Centeredness
Faith, whole-hearted
Forgiveness

O God, we use calendars extensively to set our schedules, to
remember special events, and to mark the passing of time. We
ask that you help us to use our calendars as instruments of
spiritual growth.

Remind us that a busy schedule is more oppressive than
impressive if it crowds out occasions of prayer and reflection.

Teach us to regard each dawn as the beginning of a holy day
and to identify every deed as an opportunity for serving you.

Inspire us to rejoice in the expanse of time as we live within
it and look ahead to its promised never-ending.

Giver of our daily bread, Sovereign over all eternity, we
extend to you our gratitude and praise. In the name of Jesus
Christ. Amen.

Time, stewardship of
Faithful living
Choice

Loving God, however much we profess our desire to journey in faith and to follow the course of discipleship, we must also confess to incomplete devotion and the straying of our spirits.
Forgive us, we pray.
We have turned aside from practicing reconciliation and extending mercy.
We have turned toward belief systems that trivialize your power and lifestyles that harm your creation.
We have turned down opportunities to grow in spiritual stature and explore the path of service that is the way of Christ.
We have turned back from accepting the challenge of steadfast commitment and receiving the fullness of your love and grace.
We seek your forgiveness and your guidance. Amen.

Faith, turning from
Forgiveness
General

We thank you, God, for this wondrous, ordinary day. Grant us the wisdom to unwrap the day as a gift. Engage us in opening its hours with care, prizing the people we meet within it, acknowledging you as its sender. By your grace, we will discover it to be just what we need.
Increase, we pray, our faith and faithfulness. How often we have difficulty building belief. We misuse or fail to identify the resources you provide with such loving constancy. Help us to help one another grow as persons of Spirit, as followers of the servant Christ.
We confess to complaining of your invisibility or absence. Teach us, amid our complaints, to recognize that we have turned

aside from you, that we have some spiritual blind spots, that we have a tendency to see only what we want to see.

We confess to protesting your unreachableness. Enable us, amid our protests, to confront the ways we keep you at arm's length, the ways we avoid the touch of your hand, the ways we neglect to practice the outreach that draws you close.

Forgive us. Turn our complaints into fresh visions of your love, and turn our protests into proclamations of your presence. In the name of Jesus Christ. Amen.

Common things
Grace
God, presence of

Upon our journey of faith, O God, we travel step by step. And from our first tentative tries through our continuing daily walk, we rely upon you to guide and strengthen our spirits.

We give thanks for a faith that keeps us moving. You require of us spiritual exercise, and you invite us to new places of understanding.

We give thanks for a faith that offers us challenge. By your grace, you equip us to deal with detours, dangers, and hazards of the road. By your wisdom, you do not simply remove them.

We give thanks for a faith that has direction. You call us to be wayfarers yet not wanderers. You bid us go into all the world with a decisive message of love and healing and good news.

We give thanks for a faith that draws a crowd. You offer us companionship for our journey, both in persons who share our pilgrimage and in a Savior who promises to be with us every step of the way.

We offer this prayer in the name of Jesus Christ, for it is with Christ we walk the journey of faith. Amen.

Faith, journey of
Brotherhood/Sisterhood
Jesus, as companion

God of sounds and songs, rhythms and movements, we are grateful for the music and dance that enrich our lives.

Thanks be to you for the percussive taps of a woodpecker's beak, of a carpenter's hammer.

Thanks be to you for the gracefulness of a breeze-blown willow, of a storyteller's expressive hands.

Thanks be to you for the concerts of dawn-greeting birds, of human voices blended in chorus.

Thanks be to you for the quickness of a darting damselfly, of a child's mind leaping from thought to thought.

And thanks be to you for the promise of your forgiveness and the assurance of your love. These gifts you offer to us are as music to our spirits.

We pray in the name of Jesus Christ. Amen.

Music
Gifts
Common things

O God, we meet this morning as persons who need your forgiveness, seek your love, celebrate your grace. Our spirits rejoice in acknowledging that you have created us and know us better than we know ourselves. We offer this prayer with humble thanks.

Caring God, you see the broken portions of our lives, the sharp-edged memories and the jagged emotions that cause us pain. Comfort us, we pray.

Compassionate God, you recognize the frailties of our faith, the buckling-under to injustices and the adopting of beliefs more convenient than compelling. Forgive us, we pray.

Almighty God, you affirm the fragile elements of faith, the delicate beauty of self-giving and the valuable practice of worship. Preserve us, we pray.

In the strong name of Jesus Christ, Teacher and Savior. Amen.

Brokenness
▦ Faith, fragility of
Gratitude

O God, sometimes we find it difficult to comprehend the fullness of your love for us. Throughout the whole of human history, that love has shown itself through sacrifice and steadfastness, forthrightness and forgiveness, generosity and justice. You have renewed us in times of community tragedy and personal despair. You have redeemed us from collective sin and individual misdeed. You have restored us to faithfulness when we have wandered.

We are tempted to label your love "unbelievably gracious," yet it is precisely to a firm belief in your grace that you call us. Increase our understanding, we pray. Through the communion we experience in prayer and at table, create within us open and receptive spirits. May bread and cup nourish us toward bolder commitment and clearer belief. In the name of Jesus Christ. Amen.

God, love of
▦ Grace
Communion

Loving God, we come to you bearing burdens. Some of these we identify readily; others we cannot name. Some of these seem almost a part of us; others surprise us by their presence. Some of these we carry with steady step; others break us down to a stumble or a stop. We prayerfully place all these burdens in your strong hands and ask that you do with them as you will.

We are burdened by the pressures of difficult decisions and ongoing tensions, unachieved expectations and unreleased sorrows.

We are burdened by the weight of obligations and responsibilities, workloads and schedules.

We are burdened by the heavy-heartedness of perceived failures and missed opportunities, broken relationships and shattered hopes.

Mighty and compassionate God, we pray that you bear with us and bear us up, that we might live lightly and serve well. In the name of Jesus Christ. Amen.

Burdens
God, power of
Renewal

Strong and caring God, we humbly acknowledge to you our desire to understand and our need to be understood. We come before you as seekers and supplicants. Hear our prayer.

We confess to hiding from knowledge about ourselves, to setting aside the honest criticisms of others, to evading confrontation with unseemly aspects of our thoughts and deeds. Forgive us, and move us toward bolder self-understanding.

We confess to restricting our knowledge of others, to ignoring the best within them, to allowing habit and stereotype to shape our relationships. Forgive us, and redeem our understandings of others.

We confess to limiting our knowledge of you, to avoiding serious reflection about your call to faithfulness, to regarding spiritual growth more as optional than as essential. Forgive us, and help us to understand you well.

Gracious God, in the fullness of your love, you understand us completely. Only in accepting that can we offer this prayer with confidence in the name of Jesus Christ. Amen.

Understanding
Self-deception
God, reliance upon

O God, Giver of life and Teacher of all goodness, with the opening of our eyes each morning we enter the classroom of your Spirit. Grant us the attentiveness to be able students, the persistence to follow well a course of faithfulness, the confidence to share with others the love of Christ. Equip our church to be a learning center for spiritual inquirers, for dedicated servants, for daring disciples.

Educate us to see our faith as a process and not as a possession. Provide us contact with your Word so it comes to life in the context of our experience. Move within us and among us in ways that generate deeds of compassion, commitments to justice, and visions of peace. Help us to follow, humbly and wholly, the One we call Teacher. In Jesus' name, we pray. Amen.

Education
Evangelism
Word

Loving God, in the course of our days we do much that troubles you deeply and much that is pleasing to your sight, much that reveals our faithlessness and much that proclaims our desire to honor you. Hear our prayer.

We have hidden our true feelings for unhealthy reasons of self-protection or avoidance of confrontation; we have also risked the kind of honest expression that strengthens relationships.

We have disconnected ourselves from the plight of persons victimized by injustice; we have also come to realize that love is never aloof.

We have made lifestyle choices that translate into rude treatment of your creation; we have also involved ourselves in solid efforts to preserve the wonderful world that is our home.

We have devoted scant resources of self and substance to the things we claim to value most; we have also acted upon our convictions with steadfastness and clarity.

We have displayed indifference about our spiritual health; we have also nourished ourselves on prayer and vigorously exercised our faith.

Forgive us our failings and give form to our hopes. Help us, O God, to live for you and serve you well, to be our best as followers of the One in whose name we pray. Amen.

Values
Irresponsibility 🔳
General

God of all people and places, on this World Communion Sunday we come to your table in a spirit of global community. As we join together in this meal, enable us to recognize the many ways we can serve one another.

Grant us, we pray—

• a willingness to share earth-keeping tasks
• a commitment to learning our varied histories and hopes

- a desire to engage in ecumenical activities and interfaith dialogue
- a resolve to confront injustice and to work for peace
- a determination to grow in our understanding of your Word and will

Nourish us at your table. Help us to celebrate connectedness in the human family as a sure sign of your grace. In the name of Jesus Christ. Amen.

World Communion Sunday
Community
Diversity

Loving God, we who bear Christ's name comprise a unique kind of family. We are not bound together by relationships that get charted on family trees. We cannot be identified by distinguishing family features of personality or physical appearance. We have not ever lived with one another in the closeness that is a family's fondest hope.

We are family nonetheless, and for that we offer our grateful praise.

We give thanks for the faith that bonds us together, for the spiritual heritage that has its roots in the person and work of Jesus Christ.

We give thanks for the sharing of a commitment to do your will, for the striving to act in love that serves as our identifying feature.

We give thanks for having in common a home in your creation and your eternal realm, for having a sense that all humanity is one family in your eyes.

In companionship with our brothers and sisters, we pray in Jesus' name. Amen.

Faith, family of
Community
Brotherhood/Sisterhood

Mighty and compassionate God, you have extended to us promises of presence and forgiveness, grace and understanding. Through all history, these promises have been kept with a steadfastness that inspires faithfulness and nurtures belief. So it is with grateful hearts that we pray.

Help us to be enthusiastic participants in the ongoing campaign to do your will on earth as in heaven. You have showed us what is good. Grant us the courage to let our lives be shaped by the goodness you reveal. In a world of energy-sapping frustrations and diversions from noble goals, guide us by the power and direction of your Spirit. Enable us to convey the brightness of joy to persons in grief or despair, to bring healing to those suffering illness or abuse, to make peace in the midst of tensions or conflict. Permit us to perform well those things you require of us—doing justice and loving kindness and walking humbly upon your way.

You do not ask us to cast a vote in your favor. You do ask us to commit our lives fully to your service and care. Therefore, strengthen us in spirit and faith. We pray in Jesus' name. Amen.

God, steadfastness of
Commitment
Justice

O God, you sent your Child among us to carry out a mission of love. You send us among our sisters and brothers to continue that mission always. Yet sometimes, we confess, we neglect the call.

Forgive us when we display a lack of interest in the plight of others, when the horrors of their circumstances arouse more curiosity than compassion.

Forgive us when we downplay our ability to make a difference for the better, when we act as though the strands of common humanity end at town lines or national borders.

Forgive us when we regard our outreach as optional, when we place it somewhere other than at the heart of our faith.

Forgive and redirect us, we pray, so our service might be strong and our sense of fulfillment deep. In the name of Jesus Christ. Amen.

Calling
Mission/service
Faithful living

Gracious God, you have provided us with a world abundant and balanced. You have created us a gifted people. We offer our thankful praise.

We ask also for forgiveness. The plenty of this earth remains unknown to many brothers and sisters who struggle to survive. And we know in our hearts that the problem lies less with paltriness of supply than with meagerness of will. We confess that we seldom assess our lives in terms of stewardship. We confess that we devote little effort to providing for others fair access to the basics of decent living.

We pray, too, for an expansion of appreciation. Teach us to see the gifts that are ours by grace as clear signs of your loving generosity. Help us to know in our hearts that we have been richly blessed and that you call us to creative sharing as the way of faithfulness. We confess to withholding talents that could bring joy or comfort to our brothers and sisters; we confess to ignoring our own self-worth, for we often neglect to identify ourselves as your children.

Inform our spirits. Inspire our deeds. We pray in the name of Jesus Christ. Amen.

Stewardship
Justice
Grace

Gracious and generous God, through the course of common activities and special events—the occasions of hearty companionship and honest solitude, the instances of warm conversation and earnest prayer—you reveal to us your gifts of presence and power. We deeply appreciate these gifts, for they enable us to be present for one another and to be empowered for caring action in the world.

We are thankful that you have provided us with ample resources for the good life of spiritual growth. Within the community of faith, we find persons with a wealth of experience in matters of Christian living, persons with a capacity to enrich our faith. We pray for the wisdom to cooperate with one another in sharing the treasures of our spirits. You have taught us that in the economics of faith, generosity has substantial reward, and self-giving leads to genuine fulfillment. Grant us, O God, the courage to be disciples of the One who was and is and ever shall be our Teacher. We pray in Christ's name, acknowledging Jesus Christ as Life-giver and Savior. Amen.

Stewardship
Faith, development of
Cooperation

Loving and gracious God, from whom we receive all good gifts, hear now this prayer of gratitude and praise.

We give thanks for the bounty and beauty of the earth, for lands of varied terrain and waters cupped into oceans, for summer's warm breezes and autumn's biting gusts.

We give thanks for foods crunchy and smooth, for flavors sharp and sweet, for smells that build our hunger and beckon us to table.

We give thanks for the joys of play and the satisfactions of work, for the benefits of laughter and the lessons of hard times, for the resources of experience and the opportunities of growth.

We give thanks for our own lives and for a whole human family, for love toward people as near as a hug and as far as half a world away, for friendship with creatures great and small.

We give thanks for a faith to hold, for the imagination to hope, for the desire to serve, and for the courage to act.

We offer this prayer in the name of Jesus Christ. Amen.

Thanksgiving
Common things
God, sensing

WORDS OF ASSURANCE

WORDS OF ASSURANCE

WALK DOWN any city street. Sit in any fast-food restaurant or family dining room. Attend any town meeting or church committee session. Flip on any radio or television. Go shopping at any mall. All around us, words fill the air. They reach us in a variety of volumes, accents, and tones. In them, we hear the full range of human emotions.

It does not take a statistical study to determine that many of the words we hear are negative in their impact. A significant percentage get tossed off as weapons of anger or prejudice, intended to wound and injure. Judgmental words criticize in a manner that cuts down rather than builds up. Some words reflect their speakers' numbing hopelessness or despair. Others seek to manipulate us for commercial or political purposes. Still other words babble and chatter, creating a background noise that contains little meaning.

Certainly, there are positive words as well—words of love spoken with heartfelt intent; bold and courageous words voiced in confrontation with evil; comforting words that promote healing; honest, well-considered words that seek to clarify issues or produce fresh understandings.

If, in the midst of this mix, we dare ask the question, "What's the good word?" we find that our faith generates the answer. The good word is "forgiveness," and it is conveyed during worship through "words of assurance" most often spoken by a clergyperson. This good word of forgiveness is good news to all who hear it, but in order for it to become the *best* news, it must be spoken by everyone, not just clergy. Assurance seems to be in short supply, not because God has been skimpy with forgiveness, but rather because we have been stingy in our distribution. We all long to hear words of assurance—they are so rare. But the resources of our faith are unlimited. Daily, through word and deed, we have many opportunities to affirm the reality of forgiveness, to proclaim its freeing power, to express the love of God.

The world hopes for words of assurance. The followers of Jesus Christ can fill the role of assurers. Positively. Surely.

When we unshutter our spirits, we receive a love that sets us aglow with a desire to share it as we can and as God guides us. Glory be to God. Amen.

Advent
God, love of
Faith, sharing of

God's love fills us with the longing for peace. Jesus' words and actions lead us in love's direction. The Spirit's power permits us to accomplish what love envisions. The realization of peace enters this world by the grace and power of God.

Advent
Peace
God, love of

Through the centuries, God's love has sustained the promise of Advent as a shining light upon our way. By the power and grace of our Creator, a star of hope punctures the night; the Messiah will come into this world. Glory be to God.

Advent
God, love of
Hope

Our God is gracious and self-revealing, wanting to know us and willing to be known by us. In Jesus of Nazareth, a door of understanding opened. Through the ongoing activity of the Spirit, our understanding increases.

Advent
Doors
Understanding

God's love for this world and attachment to the human family are joyfully evident in the events of Christmas. Our lives are blessed by the birth of Christ. Glory be to God.

Christmas
▣ Incarnation
Joy

Hope is a consistent sign of our Creator's presence, an indicator of the Spirit's work within us. As we bear hope into the world, we serve God well. Glory be to God.

Hope
▣ Mission/service
God, presence of

The greatness and the glory of God, the saving love of Christ, and the power of the Spirit take form in forgiveness. Receiving forgiveness, we experience closeness with God. Acknowledging it, we offer words of praise. Glory be to God.

Forgiveness
▣ God, greatness of
Praise

God lives wherever we look, listens whenever we pray, speaks in every true word, comes near as we love one another. Glory be to God.

Epiphany
▣ God, presence of
Faithful living

In working together on the fitness, health, and strength of faith, we can count on the loving encouragement of the One who called us into being. In building together a spiritual home, we connect ourselves with the Creator. Glory be to God.

Faith, development of
Home
Grace

God calls us to an unfettered faith of service in the name of Christ. We are set free by forgiveness and by the empowerment of a creative Spirit. Glory be to God.

Freedom
Empowerment
Forgiveness

At the table of Christ's family we find that there is an open welcome, an abundance of good company, and always room for more hungry people. Glory be to God.

Communion
Inclusiveness
Faith, family of

We come together to exalt our Creator, to renew ourselves for service, to share fellowship with Christ and one another. In our gathering we receive the energizing assurance of God's presence and forgiveness and love. Glory be to God.

Worship
Affirmation
Empowerment

When we offer our love to the one God and to all neighbors, we do as Christ bid, and we are graced with a feeling of true faithfulness. This is a powerful blessing we receive. All thanks and glory be to God.

Discipleship
Faithful living
Mission/service

When we reach in faith, God comes near in love. When we strive to serve in Christ's name, God consecrates our efforts. When we rely upon the Spirit's power, God fills us with a healthy trust. Glory be to God.

God, love of
Mission/service
Trust

To all who seek forgiveness through confession of sin and commitment to change, God responds with mercy and grace. Ever and always, God welcomes us home to live with joy in the world, to look with hope toward time ahead. Glory be to God.

Forgiveness
Change
God, reign of

To all who thirst, God offers access to love, mercy, and peace. Through the enactment of personal commitment and the sharing of common faithfulness, the Spirit flows in our midst. Glory be to God.

One Great Hour of Sharing
Thirst
Faithful living

We travel on the pilgrimage of faith in companionship with one another and with the Christ whose path and pace we strive to follow. And always, we are accompanied by a steadfast and enabling Spirit. Glory be to God.

Jesus, companionship of
Faith, journey of
Spirit

We are beckoned by God to live our faith as Jesus did, with dedication and with daring. And we are promised the strengthening presence of a love steadfast and enduring. Glory be to God.

Palm Sunday
Faith, call of
God, presence of

The One who gave courage to Jesus long ago promises to accompany us on the entire lifelong journey of faith. Upon straightaways, at crossroads, through difficult turns, our loving God remains steadfast and true. Glory be to God.

Palm Sunday
Faith, journey of
God, steadfastness of

The goodness of God is the news of this day, for it brings to us a forgiveness not beyond belief but rather at the heart of belief. All thanks and glory be to God.

Easter
Good news
Forgiveness

Though we often lose our senses of direction, purpose, and balance, we are never beyond the forgiving care of our Creator who remains with us to bring about the fulfillment of faith. Such is the steadfast love of God. And for it, we offer our words of praise.

Eastertide
Forgiveness
God, love of

There is no measure to the magnitude of God's love. It goes beyond all boundaries but that of grace in extending to us full forgiveness and renewal of hope. Glory be to God.

Eastertide
Grace
God, love of

In any and all circumstances, God works with wondrous power to affirm life—reconciling divisions among us, resisting evil, restoring shaken faith, renewing our spirits. Glory be to God.

Eastertide
Affirmation 🔷
God, power of

To be Christ's subjects is to discover freedom. To offer ourselves in service is to receive the grace of God. There is no greater crowning achievement in life than following the way of faith and accepting the love of our Creator. Glory be to God.

Faithful living
Freedom 🔷
Discipleship

Our growth in faith is a learning process, the drawing out of our love and the drawing forth of our service. Growth in spirit comes by grace. Glory be to God.

Faith, development of
Growth 🔷
Grace

The God of all creation cares passionately for each and every one of us. God heals and forgives, orders and restores, all so we might experience the abundance of life. Glory be to God.

God, love of
Grace 🔷
General

It is by walking in truth that we reveal love for our neighbor; it is by celebrating Christ's life that we develop a passion for freedom. These things we can do by the grace of God. These things we can do by relying on the Spirit's power. Glory be to God.

Pentecost
Neighbors
Faithful living

The One who brought into being everything that is desires the health and wholeness of all creation. Toward that end, we are granted forgiveness, supplied with hope, and renewed for the following of God's will. Glory be to God.

Wholeness
Grace
General

However we distance ourselves from God, a resurrection love embraces us. Forgiveness signals its power, and joy confirms our release. So with thanks in our hearts, let us sing our praises to God.

Forgiveness
Joy
General

Faith's great good news proclaims the presence of a God who never turns away from our needs, but ever turns toward us with an abundant and healing love. Glory be to God.

Good news
Healing
God, presence of

Above all else, God beckons us to belief, for believing activates our spirits to serve Christ through serving others. Glory be to God.

Faith, attraction of
Mission/service
Discipleship

This is the year of our Redeemer, the season of ripening faith, the day of salvation, the moment of grace. All thanks and glory be to God.

Seasons (autumn)
Time
Grace

The God who brought this world into being is the Creator of community and the One who seeks to be in communion with all humankind. Glory be to God.

World Communion Sunday
Community
Inclusiveness

Whatever inhibits community or causes separation between people, God calls us to set aside. By grace we are drawn together—as children of the earth's Creator, as persons welcome in the family of faith. Glory be to God.

Community
Faith, family of
Grace

To all whose decision it is to follow Christ and work upon building a holy habitation for humankind, God promises the resources of heaven and the companionship of believers throughout the earth. Glory be to God.

God, realm of
Community
Discipleship

The greatness of God is revealed through the bounty of forgiveness and the treasure of steadfast love. We respond to these with the gratitude of lives well lived and words of praise sung with gladness.

Stewardship
Gratitude
God, greatness of

Whenever hearts turn toward the Creator with openness and expectancy, God never fails to enter in, encouraging us always to make true thanksgiving our way of life. Glory be to God.

Thanksgiving
Openness
Faithful living

PASTORAL PRAYERS

PASTORAL PRAYERS

In CONGREGATIONAL USE, the pastoral prayer is literally the shepherd's prayer for his or her flock. It demands of the one who is praying a shepherd-like vigilance and an awareness of the flock's needs. Are any members of the flock wandering off in unsafe directions? Are there any hurt or ill? What dangers threaten or fears distress them? What nourishment and guidance do they need? Those questions are serious ones that require tending to in prayer. Yet pastoral prayer strays from its purpose if, instead of expressing concerns, the speaker imposes answers. The authority of a pastor-shepherd derives from a commitment to caretaking and, ultimately, to trusting reliance upon the leadings of the One known as the Good Shepherd.

The humble, noble task of caretaking is one our faith beckons us to assume—taking on the cares of persons burdened or oppressed, taking care of those who need support or assistance, taking care to be compassionate and forthright in all our dealings with others. It is unfortunate that the phrase "Take care" is now used as unreflectively and offhandedly as "Have a nice day." How great it would be to reclaim the phrase, to hear it remind us of our calling, and to allow it to direct our actions.

In the pastoral prayers of public worship, we often ask God to take care of the persons and situations we identify. We do so with confidence that God will tend to matters. As we offer our private prayers, it is absolutely fitting that they also assume a pastoral tone. All of us have persons in our lives for whom we feel a responsibility, persons whose welfare we seek and whose well-being we strive to promote. Over time, as faith matures, we experience a change in our sense of who belongs in this flock charged to our care. The flock becomes more extensive. We might well expect this, for the Good Shepherd who bid us pray for enemies

111

and practice hospitality toward strangers commended an inclusive kind of caretaking, an expansive kind of prayer-making. In these two ventures of faith, we are pastoral partners with God and with one another.

God of all creation, we offer our prayer today for this church, not out of parochial concerns but rather with passionate hopes.

We give thanks, first and foremost, for your presence and your promise of empowerment. By our strength and resources alone we cannot accomplish even a small portion of what we are capable of doing; we become dispirited, and the good news is less than fervently conveyed. But by your grace, the Spirit can renew us, giving energy and direction. We ask that you help us become an ever more joyous servant people. Through the exercise of love, make us more fit in faith and fellowship.

Enable us in the future, as you have in the past, to be a caring congregation—persons who struggle with complex issues in seeking your will, persons who sense the need to be stewards of the good earth, persons who risk outreach, persons who dare to share deeply with one another.

Uniting now in silent prayers of supplication and thanksgiving, we continue our worship. [*Allow time for silent prayer.*]

We pray in the name of Jesus Christ. Amen.

Advent
Empowerment
Gratitude

O God, on this final Sunday of the Advent season, we look around and see in holiday decorations visible signs of the joy we feel within. We see the story portrayed by children and hearken back in memory to our own childhood days and celebrations different in form but not in feeling. We give voice to carols that warm the chilliest of spirits like a cocoa cup in wintered hands. We anticipate your coming and give silent thanks.

In days ahead, help us toward a growing understanding of just what Christ's coming among us means for every moment of life.

Fill us with the joy of receiving a great and surprising gift.

Inspire us to speak with the wonder of children.

Enable us to proclaim and sing your praises beyond the holidays.

Grant us the courage to be makers of peace whenever and wherever we can.

We pray that the love shown through your presence moves us to love in response. To all our friends and neighbors, brothers and sisters, who yearn to feel the touch of love, let us come bearing within us the Christ who came as a babe and who grew to teach the prayer we share together saying: [*The Prayer of Jesus*]. Amen.

Advent
Faith, inclusiveness of
Responsiveness

O God, your entrance into this world amazes us with its gentle power. The child of Mary, infant sign of your infinite love, seems as a solitary candle in the vastness of night or as a single breath of warmth in a world chilled by separateness and uncaring. Yet tonight we celebrate, for the words of the prophet Isaiah have borne true—"the people [now] have seen a great light." And we celebrate because your love revealed in Christ possesses the power to thaw any coldness of heart.

How grateful we are that your light penetrated into human history in that Bethlehem stable. Then and there, you hallowed the humble of spirit and of means. You coupled the ordinary and the sacred. You identified the joy and wonder of being surprised by grace.

We pray on this Christmas Eve that, wherever there is gloom of situation or dimness of hope, our faith might shine. And we ask that when our own bright ideas seem to us far better than flickering faith, you turn us toward Christ as the source of true illumination and set our spirits aflame.

We will leave this place tonight with thanks in our hearts, for with the birth of your Son a light dawned that cannot be extinguished. As we pass the candle flame from hand to hand, may we sense deep within our being the contagious, continuous quality of our faith. May we depart kindled in spirit, light-bearers to the world. In the name of our Savior, Jesus Christ, Amen.

Christmas Eve (Candlelight)
Light
Mission/service

Loving God, we feel the excitement of this season as it touches us in the warm greetings of friends, as it dazzles us with ornaments and lights, as it enfolds us in the verses of carols, as it opens us to hearing afresh the story of Jesus' birth. Our gratitude is deep.

We give thanks for Christmas love—for its origins in a humble stable, for its expansion throughout the world, for its embrace of all persons, for its effect upon our lives as a generator of renewal and encouragement.

We give thanks for Christmas gladness—for its source in a baby's birth, for its durability through all the centuries, for its community-building character, for its capacity to deliver cheer and healing amid frightening or discouraging circumstances.

We give thanks for Christmas hope—for its beginning as a guiding star, for its constancy through all of history, for its bold imagining and envisioning of a finer world, for its power to bring about miraculous faithfulness in us and in others.

We celebrate this evening the birth of Christ and offer our prayer in Christ's name. Amen.

Christmas Eve
Hope
Gratitude

O God, it is perhaps on Christmas Day that your power and love most take hold of us. We offer this prayer acknowledging you as our source of help and hope.

We pray, O God, for your good earth and its inhabitants. Charge us with a reverence for all life within your creation. Instill in the leaders and peoples of the world a spirit of cooperation and respect. Strengthen the channels, structures, and efforts that can bring the entire human family into an age of peace and understanding, justice and sharing.

We pray, O God, for families of all kinds. Support them with the presence of One who was born into a family and who is called Counselor as well as Holy Child. Renew in our relationships with others the valuing of commitment, gentleness, and acceptance. Grant that we might be persons who seek more to give than to take, more to respect than to demand, more to appreciate than to complain, more to love than to ignore.

Be near us as we experience individually the troughs and crests of life. Help us to realize that our worth as persons is not something we can generate or produce but is rather a gift of grace, a holy consequence of our creation by your hand. Enable us in good times to give praise with exuberance and in bad times to rely upon you with faith. We have yet to know fully the extent of your encouragement, the scope of your healing . . . there is far more for us to entrust to your power.

We pray as Christmas people whom you have reached out and touched through the birth of Jesus Christ. We have felt the power of your promise and your presence. In remembering the wondrous birth in Bethlehem and the miraculous growth of belief, we come before you now as people filled with hope and poised to serve.

Our prayer is offered in the name of that Child whose words of later years we now share, saying: [*The Prayer of Jesus*]. Amen.

Christmas
World
Commitment

Loving God, during this holiday season our days are enlivened by glad sounds of carols, warm exchanges of welcoming words, light laughter of children at play, kitchen clatters of preparation and clean-up, easy-chair sighs and snores. These are the sounds of our common life, a life made holy by the presence of your Child within it, and for them we give our thanks. Hear our thankfulness, too, for the times when we capture some silence, when we savor those elusive quiet times of settled spirits. Beckon us toward prayer in those moments that are still. And help us to balance celebration and contemplation, activity and reflection.

We look back on a year of great changes in the world, perhaps great changes in ourselves. And we look ahead to hopes well formed and recorded, as well as to hopes yet unimagined. In our anticipation, we trust in your steadfastness and love.

So much we can bring to you in prayer—personal problems and family issues and needs of neighbors, concerns for people neglected in this nation and for those entrapped by hostilities in _____ and _____.
Gracious God, listener to all prayer, hear us now as we speak with you in silence. [*Allow time for silent prayer.*]

We pray in the name of Jesus Christ. Amen.

Christmastide
New Year
God, trust in

O God, we come before you as individuals with varied feelings. We are persons joyful and sorrowful, morose and content, angry and serene, despondent and hopeful. Because you are great and caring, you hold each one of us gently in your hands, and you minister to us according to our need. We thank you for your personal touch and your steadfast compassion.

Loving Sovereign, we also come before you as a gathered people, a community. And today, in this first worship service of a new year, we offer special thanks that you have made us a people who congregate. How good it is to hear the voices of brothers and sisters raised in song, to know that our dependence upon your power is one that is shared with our neighbors, to sense the energy of a connectedness generated by mutual faith.

For your presence in each life, for your support of our life together, we give thanks in the name of Jesus Christ. Amen.

New Year
Community
God, compassion of

O, God, because we identify ourselves with the name of your Child, we ask that you equip us and charge us to be faithful people whose actions in the world are consistent with an attitude of worship, whose deeds witness to the power of Christ's love. You call us to carry that love within, to bear it into the world. Grant us the patience and strength to undergo the labors of love that give birth to Christian hope.

Let the imaginations of our hearts be as daring as those within our minds. Lead us to risk enacting the wisdom of the Spirit, to assert the reality of your reign in the midst of this world.

Fill us with aspirations that guide us toward reaching our individual potentials, serving you with gladness, working toward justice and peace for all people.

Enable us to envision a future responsive to your presence, suitable as a dwelling-place for your human family.

In our communion this day and our commitment through days ahead, we open ourselves to your Spirit and pray in the name of Jesus Christ. Amen.

Witnessing
Risk
Communion

O God, we offer this morning a simple prayer.

We pray for the world—that its leaders consider in all decisions what is right and just; that its people, so long separated from one another, work toward reunion of the human family.

We pray for your church—that its worship honor you and its deeds please you; that the people within it act with joy and courage.

We pray for those who hurt—that physical ills receive the kind of healing only your Spirit can give; that emotional distress and relational turmoils be touched by your calming, settling hand.

We pray for children everywhere—that they may have a future; that their capacity for wonder and their tendency toward trust become models for our faith.

We pray that you strengthen us to make wise life decisions so we can participate in the processes of reconciling, building, healing, and hoping. Our prayers are offered in the name of Jesus Christ. Amen.

Simplicity
World
Healing

Loving God, we give hearty thanks for a faith that lifts us, that can get us hope-filled and Spirit-borne. In a world of hands that push us down and point when we fall, the church family is called to extend hands that offer able assistance and reach out in the activity of prayer. For this call to counter the world's unkindness with a bold Christly compassion, we offer our gratitude and praise.

For many in our community, the recent past has been a time of trial and difficult decision. There have been strains and stumbles. We pray that by your power those things that seem to be falling apart in people's lives begin to fall into place. Work your grace in our midst as bringer of stability and serenity, insight and healing.

As we share the holy communion today, grant us a special awareness of our brothers and sisters around the world. Help us in the future to meet their hunger for your Word, their thirst for justice. May our relations with them truly embody the love of Christ through an outpouring of deeds of mercy.

Hear our prayer offered in Jesus' name. Amen.

Compassion
Communion
Faith, family of

Loving God, we give you thanks for the beauty of a dawning day, and for the way it dawns upon us in quiet times or through community contacts that we need and have your steadfast presence in our lives.

We give thanks for warming weather that draws us outside, and for the warmth of fellowship that draws out the kindness and joy within us.

We give thanks for new life springing up around us, and for the possibilities of new life that come to bud in forgiveness and blossom in service.

We give thanks for the voices of creation that herald a season of renewal, and for the capacity we have through speaking and giving to voice our support for persons in need.

We give thanks also for the silence that opens to those who seek an entrance into prayer. Hear us as we express our concerns and hopes in silence. [*Allow time for silent prayer.*]

We pray in the name of Jesus Christ, whose own prayer we share, saying: [*The Prayer of Jesus*]. Amen.

One Great Hour of Sharing
Seasons (spring)
Renewal

Loving God, we aspire to be bearers of light in this world. Whenever deeds of violence or injustice cloud over hopes, and whenever individual suffering or corporate pain threaten to enshroud, help us to hold the bright presence of Christ above the horizon for all humankind to see.

We aspire to lead faithful lives. Grant us the courage that requires, for the gospel beckons us to do much that others will regard as foolish—to serve selflessly, to love unconditionally, to forgive entirely. Strengthen our resolve to become fools for the sake of Christ, persons who dare to confront this world with acts of spiritual sanity that extend your wondrous good news.

Within our hearts and minds, we have concerns for persons close to us, for situations that draw from us the compassion of our faith. Hear now as we pour them out to you in the fullness and the emptiness of our silent prayer. [*Allow time for silent prayer.*]

We give thanks for your gracious responsiveness and offer now the prayer our Savior bid us pray together, saying: [*The Prayer of Jesus*]. Amen

Lent
Hope
Faith, foolishness of

O God, you call us to reflection and action. You bid us to be silent before you and to offer words of praise. You enable us to use our solitude well and you encourage us to be in communion with all humanity. Help us to be faithful, and throughout the Lenten season may we attune our wills to yours. We pray in the name of Jesus Christ, who invited us to share this prayer, saying: [*The Prayer of Jesus*]. Amen.

Ash Wednesday
Reflection
Faithful living

O God, we come to you with simple words of prayer.

We seek clarity of thought and depth of feeling in all we do; grant us clear minds and open sensitivity.

For persons in our families or community beset by illness—[*mention names*]—we ask comfort, healing, and understanding; allow us to be bearers of wholeness to those who struggle.

For individuals or families facing trying times, upcoming operations, or hard decisions, we offer ourselves as support and pray for your Spirit's guidance and comfort.

For those who have experienced loss—loss of a family member or friend, loss of confidence, loss of direction—we ask that new strength be found and a capacity for renewal be developed.

For persons throughout the world who hunger and thirst for food or justice, enable a satisfaction and a fulfillment. For those engaged in conflict or victimized by war, we ask that adversaries become allies, that the building of peace become a valued vocation, that the hurt disappear.

We pray in Jesus' name, Amen.

Lent
Healing
General

O God, as we enter Holy Week, we ask for an openness of spirit.

Attune us to Jesus' teachings in a way that helps us understand why his words, in their fullness of love and truth, are yet so threatening to those who wield this world's power, to those who entrust their futures to anything or anyone other than to you, our Creator and Sustainer.

Enable us to move through this week as though we do not know what lies ahead. Let us feel its drama full force so there might be a freshness to our insights and our wonder.

For today, charge us with the triumph of a stunning moment in the history of our faith. fill us with visions of a world ruled by that humble carpenter from Nazareth who is also Ruler of all creation. Inspire the imagination of our faith. What form does your realm take, O God? How will you use us to build it? Dare we rely on your love, a power at odds with the powers of the world? With such questions we open ourselves as seekers, and we submit ourselves as followers to the One whose prayer we share together, saying: [*The Prayer of Jesus*]. Amen.

Palm Sunday
Faith, subversiveness of
God, realm of

Loving God, on this day of remembrance and celebration, this entry into the week we call Holy, we pray that a continuing and constant spirit of openness condition our growing faith. We welcome you into our lives and invite you to inhabit our hearts and inspire our actions.

Grant us the courage to be followers more than fans of Jesus Christ. We realize it is infinitely easier to wave palms on a day of high emotion and popular support than it is to profess allegiance when the cross looms large and popularity wanes. Give us a spiritual steadfastness that enables us to follow the course of Christ wherever it leads.

Forgive us when we behave more like a crowd of observers than a congregation of believers. We confess that there are times our faith seems as external to us as a passing parade and we function as spiritual spectators. Involve us in our beliefs, O God, so we might participate in a mutual ministry, with Christ and one another, serving you with purpose and with passion.

Help us in the week ahead to keep in our prayers especially those for whom Jesus displayed a keen concern—the poor, the distressed, the victims of injustice, the spiritually bereft, the ill, the neglected or rejected. Charge us to keep pace with our Savior through triumph and trial, praying always in Jesus' name, and now in the words Jesus taught us, saying: [*The Prayer of Jesus*]. Amen.

Palm Sunday
Discipleship
Risk

Loving God, it is because of this day that we designate the week gone by as Holy. How much we have learned through the resurrection of Jesus Christ, for that event reveals to us the extensiveness of your grace, the breadth of your forgiveness, the limitlessness of your power, and the passion of your love for humankind.

We pray that our faith be enriched and energized daily by prayerful contact with the risen Christ. And we ask that you guide us toward the way of resurrection living.

When we are despondent or grieving, bereft of hope or mourning loss, grant us visions of new opportunities and appreciations of past gifts.

When we feel emptiness within certain portions of our being or a lack of resources for the task at hand, remind us that an empty tomb is the sign of new life and that your Spirit is ever-resourceful.

When our brothers and sisters hunger for justice or sustenance, help us to claim our Christly roles as table-setters and servants, offerers of the Bread of Life in all its forms.

When our brothers and sisters need the comfort of connection with caring people, enable us to reach out in fellowship to reveal the joy of companionship with Christ.

We pray now in the name of the One whose resurrection we celebrate and whose words we share, saying: [*The Prayer of Jesus*]. Amen.

Easter
Commitment
God, power of

O God, we offer our prayer this morning for the world you brought into being, the world you love—

We pray for sustenance, not only the vital products of labor and harvest, but also the flowering hopes that envision a more beautiful future and the ripening compassion that brings it to fruition.

We pray for patience that builds connections among people over time and that enables new understandings to form upon carefully constructed foundations.

We pray for urgency in our actions to preserve creation, to create a world unpolluted by chemicals of convenience, weapons of destruction, waste items of greedy consumption.

We pray for resiliency, the kind your Spirit can provide to all persons experiencing transitions of job or place or circumstance.

We pray for love to fill us, to guide us, to permeate our lives as a source of inspiration.

Giving our thanks for your potent presence among us, we continue with the words Jesus taught us saying: [*The Prayer of Jesus*]. Amen.

Environment
Faith, components of ▨
Community

Loving God, you have been as a parent to us, and for that we give thanks.

You birthed into being all humanity, called us together as a family, and nurtured us through trying times into a present filled with hope.

You have been our homemaker, granting us the earth and reminding us when we mess it up that it is one of our family responsibilities to care for it.

You love us with a steadfastness that we count on and cherish, for we always find you willing to listen and to share a wisdom born of experience and filled with insight.

You are our source of strength, our guide in times of decision, our motivator to act against injustice and to build a community of caring.

We give thanks this morning for mothers throughout the world, for the mothers who are our own. We pray that your love embrace all mothers: the mothers of the disappeared in South America and Mothers Against Drunk Driving, mothers who bond together to struggle for peace and mothers who care for children with AIDS, mothers who work in the home and mothers who maintain the delicate balance of career and family life, mothers who parent in cooperation with a father and mothers going it alone.

Hear our prayer offered in the name of Jesus Christ, whose mother lived her faith boldly. Amen.

Justice
Mothers
God, attributes of

Ever-engaging and ever-renewing God, on Pentecost long ago you startled the followers of Christ with a gracious and glorious gift of Spirit. It came as the rush of a mighty wind, as the flicker and flame of fire, as the power that transforms conversation into true communication. Enter again into our midst, into the comings and goings, the dealings and doings of our daily lives.

When our faith is becalmed by idleness or indifference, let your Spirit propel us. As we open ourselves to the insights of your Word, set us on a course of service.

When our faith lacks energy, let your Spirit fire it up. Turn us toward the tasks of reaching out to the rejected and healing the broken-hearted, toward the goals of preserving your good earth and making it humanity's haven.

When our faith speaks a language few understand, let your Spirit provide a common tongue. Help us proclaim the good news with a clarity of speech and deed that leads to dialogue and partnership and cooperation among your people.

Now we come to you in silent prayer, trusting that the concerns we carry, the hopes we hold, the yearnings we confess will be accepted and acted upon by the Spirit's power. [*Allow time for silent prayer.*] In the name of Jesus Christ, we pray. Amen.

Pentecost
Faithful living
Commitment

Loving God, on this day of Pentecost, we celebrate that occasion long ago when people of many nations and regions, feeling the presence of your Spirit, came to understand one another. Help us, we pray, in a world of strident animosities and reluctant cooperation, long-standing hatreds and ongoing conflicts, to exercise the power you give us to build understanding. Grant that the church serve as a bridge of reconciliation between persons who focus more on their differences than on their common humanity.

Gracious God, on this day of confirmation, we ask that you fill us with the wisdom and courage to confirm the faith that draws us—each and every one of us—together. When our commitment has more the character of convenience than of loving purpose, strengthen us. Restore any infirm faith to full and energetic health so we might serve well as you guide us through time.

We offer our prayer in hope and in the name of Jesus Christ whose words we share saying: [*The Prayer of Jesus*]. Amen.

Pentecost
Confirmation
Understanding

Loving God, for times that are alive with a feeling of friendship and a sense of community, we give you thanks. Work within us and among us that we move from gratitude to deeds of mercy and justice.

For the moments in our lives, however fleeting they may be, when we are struck by childlike wonder or are amazed by an insight born anew in our spirits, we give you thanks. Turn our perceptions into the practices of faith.

For extended periods of contact with you, through quiet prayer alone or active ministries to those in need, we give you thanks. Draw us into forms of worship and service that will sustain us.

As children in your family, we give thanks for sisters and brothers throughout the earth, and we close our simple prayer with the words of One who binds us close to one another and to you, saying: [*The Prayer of Jesus*]. Amen.

Faithful living
Gratitude
Community

O God, we offer a prayer of thanks for love. We acknowledge you as its Source and Creator, and our gratitude is great.

Thank you for the imagination of love that enables us always to envision a world more kind, more just, more peaceful.

Thank you for the opportunities to love, for you bid us have not only an active imagination but an enacting one that puts faithfulness into deeds.

Thank you for the tenderness of love that brings comfort and healing to harsh places of dispiritedness and physical ills.

Thank you for the power of love generated by your grace and forgiveness, a power that accomplishes through us what we consider impossible, that gives us courage to serve unselfishly.

Our thanks is deep. Hear now our silent prayer for those persons and situations in need of your love and our concern. [*Allow time for silent prayer.*]

We pray in the name of Jesus Christ. Amen.

God, love of
Gratitude
Compassion

Loving God, you have given us the capacity to sing, and we pray that you allow our appreciation of music to guide us in the ways of faith.

Help us to listen gratefully to the tunes that abound in the natural world, to understand them as praise directed to you—the songs of wetland and forest, the music of the spheres.

Grant us a sensitivity for hearing the lifesongs of our brothers and sisters, especially when the rhythms of their experiences differ from ours, when the melodies are plaintive or sorrowful.

Urge us to approach each day as an opportunity to sing the song in our hearts, to express our faith in a tone of spiritual celebration.

Encourage us, in a world that urges us toward loud-voiced solos, to honor your presence in our midst with the seeking of harmony, with the building of community.

Offering thanks for your steadfast love, we pray in the name of Jesus Christ. Amen.

Music
Joy
Community

O God, we are many and we are one. Grant that our variety be understood and used as a means of serving you with united purpose.

We differ in the skills we have to offer, in the concerns that are foremost in our hearts, in the ways we were brought up. We vary in our political points of view, in our private hopes and fears, and in our attitudes and approaches, yet we are one in the Spirit. Help us to perceive that unity and receive it as a gift. Remind us that, although this does not make us the same, it does enable us, if we open our eyes, to see the connectedness among us at the spiritual level. And it does enable us, if we open our hearts, to make acts of love and compassion a priority.

Through all changes in our life together may we all be one—in our allegiance to you above all, our trust in you in every circumstance, our hope in you alone.

Hear our prayer offered in the name of Jesus Christ, whose own prayer we share, saying: [*The Prayer of Jesus*]. Amen.

Reformation Sunday
Diversity
Unity, spiritual

Loving God, in our gathering together for worship, we have a special opportunity to give you thanks, an occasion for reflecting as a community upon those things that evoke our gratitude. We pray that this might be a practice place for thankfulness, that the sensitivity to your grace gained here be an inspiration for generous spirits. By virtue of our many common needs and concerns, we can unite in voicing our thanksgiving through prayer and song. But you have also blessed us individually in ways unique and often unseen, ways that move us now to become a congregation bound together in silent expressions of prayerful gratitude. Hear us as we offer our quiet thanks. [*Allow time for silent prayer.*]

In the name of Jesus Christ, for whom we give thanks always, we pray these words, saying: [*The Prayer of Jesus*]. Amen.

Stewardship
Gratitude
God, generosity of

God of all people, we ask this morning that you inspire us to look hard at the ways we inhabit the world you formed and entrusted to our care. There are unnatural clouds in the air, unheeded cries across the continents, unseemly curtailments of freedom, unconscionable calls to arms, unimaginable crises brooding in human hearts. This is not an environment in which children thrive, so as we bow our heads we may sense the weight of a millstone about our necks.

Yet by your grace and through the power of your love, a power generated by resurrection faith, we cannot sink into despair. You are a God who offers promise and possibility; you are a God who requires dedication and daring. So grant us a vision of a world hospitable to all humanity's children; so strengthen us to build such a world moment by moment, deed by deed, hope by hope.

Beyond mis-speakings and deceptions, fractional and fractured truths, may we come to live by the Christly standard of honesty that leads us to speak the truth in love.

Beyond commitment to unquestioned authority, rigid rules and orders, may we come to live out of commitments that are at once the products of critical thought and Christly conscience.

Beyond preparing for personal or intergroup conflicts in a manner that almost assures their emergence, may we come to prepare for reconciliations that evolve peace by peace.

Hear our prayers offered in the name of your Child, Jesus Christ, whose prayer we share, saying: [*The Prayer of Jesus*]. Amen.

Environment
Justice
Commitment

Loving God, we give thanks that you are an active and ardent seeker of your people. Grant that in our exercise of compassion, our dedication to justice, our commitment to practice a Christly love, we might be filled with a Spirited persistence.

We offer our prayers this morning for all who suffer—

• for relatives and friends of persons involved in sudden accident or prolonged illness
• for the homeless of our world, refugees in crowded camps or street-dwellers in cities
• for those malnourished in body, mind, or spirit
• for persons held captive by addiction to destructive substances or behaviors
• for individuals and groups still victimized by prejudices subtle or blatant
• for people entrapped in conflicts contrived by the power-hungry or driven by blind ideology
• for those hurt by our own neglect or misdeed
• for others we name to you in silence [*Allow silent time.*]

O God, you will for your children peace and wholeness and joy that come from sharing the kind of love you extend to us. Help us as we seek to serve in the name of Jesus Christ, who voiced our gratitude and our hopes when he taught us to pray, saying: [*The Prayer of Jesus*]. Amen.

Compassion
Justice
General

Your participation in the pastoral prayer is invited. Each time you hear the phrase, "and to this purpose," please respond with the words, "We dedicate ourselves, O God." Let us pray.

Loving God, we know you to be the Creator of all that is and Parent to humankind, to be our compassionate Provider of guidance and support. We seek to honor you in worship, and to this purpose . . .

We dedicate ourselves, O God.

Reconciling God, we acknowledge that you come into our midst to bond us to our brothers and sisters, to nurture our sense of shared heritage and common ground. We work to build a ministry of mutuality and trust, and to this purpose . . .

We dedicate ourselves, O God.

Inspiring God, we hear your call to enact faith with conviction and courage, to address situations where peace is fractured, justice disregarded, innocence abused, or creation harmed. We strive to speak your Word through our deeds, and to this purpose . . .

We dedicate ourselves, O God.

Transforming God, we recognize the need for changes in our systems and shifts in our outlooks, for renovation of our spirits and restructuring of our priorities. We aspire to be, like the disciples of early Christian times, people who "turn the world upside down," and to this purpose . . .

We dedicate ourselves, O God.

Enduring God, we give thanks that through the years you have dealt with us mercifully and generously, and that for all eternity we have your promise of forgiveness and grace. We desire to express our gratitude always, and to this purpose . . .

We dedicate ourselves, O God.

We offer this prayer in the name of our church's founder, Jesus Christ, whose words we say together in one voice: [*The Prayer of Jesus*]. Amen.

Commitment
God, attributes of
Church

PRAYERS OF DEDICATION

PRAYERS OF DEDICATION

MANY OF US recall being brought up to say "thank you" at appropriate times and to fire off thank-you notes with courteous promptness. Although we sometimes had to be coerced into proper expressions of thankfulness, the repeated practice helped us develop some semblance of a healthy "gratitude-attitude." Given the freedoms of adulthood, we may get a bit lax in responding to gifts, kindnesses, favors. We may even find ourselves—with considerable support from our culture—naming what we have earned and what we have deserved far more readily than identifying all the unrequested and unmerited gifts that are ours by the grace of God.

Children at a certain stage of development often have a fondness for using the word "mine" in such a way as to claim possession of just about everything in their environment. They might point at the moon and say, "Mine!" A package just delivered—"Mine!" A sibling's toy—"Mine!" We try to train children away from this possessiveness, or at least teach them to discern and respect the claims of others. However, most adults are very much like those children in their sweeping assertions of ownership. We might point to a house or a car and say, "Mine!" A bank account—"Mine!" A person in a relationship that is taken for granted—"Mine!"

Our tendency toward aggressive possessiveness permits little space for acknowledging the grace of God. We grab hold of everything we can get and seldom give thanks to the Giver. How spiritually helpful it would be if, every time we used the word "mine," we were to substitute the word "God's." That practice would help us to redefine ourselves as stewards rather than owners, and it would lead us toward prayers of genuine gratitude.

We find God's grace difficult to accept, but the simple truth is this: all that we have is ours by the grace of God. When the apostle Paul advised the Thessalonians to "pray constantly," he was urging them to adopt a faith-based lifestyle, one marked by attentive appreciation and awareness of God's grace. That lifestyle is one we are wise to choose, for it leads to spiritual fulfillment. And it leads to dedication, in prayer and vision and action. Each moment becomes a thank-you note to our gracious, all-giving God.

Gracious God, you use what seems to be small change in the treasury of this world to make great changes in the lives of your people. By the power of your love, you magnify our gifts. So we pray with grateful hearts and with spirits growing in generosity. We await the coming anew of the Christmas Child, our beloved servant Savior. Amen.

Advent
Change
Generosity

Powerful God, through the work funded by these offerings, may we participate in bringing the light of your love to those who dwell amid pain or sorrow. Use our gifts to brighten persons depressed or grieving, to enlighten persons seeking wisdom and grace, to energize persons building justice and peace. We pray in Jesus' name. Amen.

Advent
Light
God, power of

Loving God, you entered this world long ago in the person of a Child born in an obscure village to peasant parents. Today we honor those humble origins as a sign of your greatness, we receive the Child as our Savior, and we regard the presence of Jesus to be as near as the moment at hand. In response to your gift of the Christ-child, we present our offerings of honest earnings and earnest commitments. Amen.

Christmas
◈ God, presence of
Commitment

Loving and leading God, we are grateful for a faith in which practicing generosity is an indication of wisdom, making peace is a mark of power, and serving others is a sign of freedom. We express our faith through the way that we live and through these offerings that we give. Receive us and our gifts. We pray in Jesus' name. Amen.

Christmastide
◈ Wisdom
Peace

Loving God, you transform the coin of this world into the currency of your realm. May love, enacted through the church, become the legal tender of our life together, and may we spend it with Spirited joy in the name of Jesus Christ. Amen.

Christmastide
◈ God, realm of
Church

Gracious God, may the gifts in these plates be as hearty servings of earnest hope and generous helpings of enacted faith. Through their use in the ministry of this church, may your will be done. We pray in the name of Jesus Christ, whose life nourished our life. Amen.

Generosity
Hope
Communion

O God, help us to resist any temptation to settle for a church that is merely viable. Enable us to build a church that ministers with a vital presence and power. Toward this project of construction, we offer our contributions and our commitment. In the name of Jesus Christ. Amen.

Church
Commitment
Mission/service

O God, we give from our earnings so the church might be strengthened. And we pray that the yearnings of faith take full form in devoted worship, caring mission, extensive education, and brave witness. Use our offerings and our actions to accomplish your will within the world. In Jesus' name, we pray. Amen.

God, will of
Church
General

Loving God, you permit us in worship to collect our thoughts and feelings, then focus them in prayer. You encourage us in worship to collect our offerings and intentions, then release them for your use. We ask that you receive our prayer and guide the use of all our gifts. In the name of Jesus Christ, we pray. Amen.

Worship
Gifts
General

O God, we often affirm our love for others by presentations of gifts and by vows of commitment. Receive these offerings as sincere affirmations of our love for you. Put to holy use our giftedness and our committed lives. In the name of Jesus Christ, we pray. Amen.

God, love for
Affirmation
Commitment

Loving God, may our sense of belonging within a community of faith nurture the longing to be your faithful servants. Teach us to build a partnership with your Spirit that advances the ways of generosity and grace. Accept our giving and receive our gifts. We pray in Jesus' name. Amen.

Mission/service
Spirit
Community

Loving God, you have invested in humankind the saving life of Christ and the valuable presence of your Spirit. We return to you an offering of interest extended in the form of devotion to worship, dedication to service, and commitment to generosity. Accept our gifts, we pray, and use them to expand the ministry of Jesus Christ, in whose name we pray. Amen.

God, love of
Salvation
Devotion

Loving God, we place our offerings in these plates, we place our faith in you, we place our confidence in the Spirit's power, and we place our hope in the ongoing work of Christ's church. Accept our gifts and our gratitude. We pray in Jesus' name. Amen.

Church
Hope
General

Loving God, as we celebrate Jesus' entry into Jerusalem and into our lives, we offer these gifts as expressions of praise and signs of welcoming spirits. Use what we give to pave the way for your work in the world, to encourage the church to stride forth proclaiming your love for all humanity. We pray humbly and confidently in our Savior's name. Amen.

Palm Sunday
Praise
God, love of

Loving God, through the resurrection you express a forgiveness grand and generous, and you affirm the value of life in a manner both gracious and bold. As recipients of your forgiveness, we offer these gifts with heartfelt thanks. Use them, we pray, to serve those in material distress, and to inspire in ourselves and others a renewal of spiritual vitality. Life-giving God, accept our gifts and our gratitude. In the name of Jesus Christ. Amen.

Easter
Forgiveness
Renewal

God of new life, you teach us that our faith is forgiving and for giving. Inspire us to expand our faith through reconciling deeds and to expend it through generous offerings. Accept these gifts, we pray, as signs of our desire to serve well in the name of Jesus Christ. Amen.

Eastertide
Faith, deeds of
Forgiveness

Great and gracious God, though we offer our prayers in secret and refrain from publicizing our giving, we ask that you encourage us to make visible our faith. May our deeds serve as enacted prayers and our giving bear witness to your abundant love. In the name of Jesus Christ. Amen.

Eastertide
Humility
Faithful living

O God, we give thanks that the life of this church body is marked by more than an accumulation of years. We have acquired from you a sense of vision and purpose for ministry in this place. Through many generations, you have guided us to expend love generously, to give to others as Christ gave to us. You have granted us growth as a congregation. This day of celebration, we offer our gifts with gratitude and praise. In Jesus' name. Amen.

Church, anniversary
Mission/service
Gratitude

Loving God, we ask that you inspire in us a way of giving that makes it much more than an automatic deposit in a passing plate. fill us with your Spirit that we might truly offer ourselves as gifts. Weaken any false allegiances we might have, and strengthen our commitment to you. Deepen our understanding of your love's leadings, and heighten our awareness of every neighbor's needs. As followers of Jesus seeking to grow in grace and generosity, we pray in our Savior's name. Amen.

Dedication
Commitment
Self-giving

Time that is precious and money we have earned,
Talents that fill us and skills we have learned—
These are a few of our favorite things.
O God, may we offer to you our favorite and our best, and may all our gifts and our giving be acceptable in your sight. In Jesus' name. Amen.

Common things
Self-giving
General

Loving God, in letting go of the gifts we offer, in releasing them for your use through the church, help us to let go of any attempts or inclinations to control your activity in our lives. We pray for the reign in our midst of your free and graceful Spirit. In the name of Jesus Christ. Amen.

Freedom
Spirit
God, reign of

Loving God, through all our years, let the church be a place where we learn about love and practice it, where we envision peace and work to build it, where we meet partners in faith and cherish them, where we discover our gifts and offer them. May your Spirit guide us toward joy and generosity. In Jesus' name we pray. Amen.

Pentecost
Church
Peace

Loving God, you bid us take stock of our actions and bond ourselves to your will. You call us to invest our lives in Christian discipleship and service. You invite us to give generously in support of persons in need. As we make these offerings, we give thanks for a faith that asks much and that yields an abundance beyond measure. In Jesus' name. Amen.

Discipleship
Faith, as investment
Abundance

Ever-creating and ever-renewing God, we know your love as a resource that cannot be depleted. Grounding our faith in that knowledge, and relying upon the companionship of Christ and the sustenance of your Spirit, we give freely, generously, and gladly. In the name of Jesus Christ. Amen.

God, as Creator
Renewal
General

Gracious God, help us to appreciate how much we profit from the discipline of giving and how much we gain by expending ourselves in Christly love. Enable us to offer to you what we value most. In Jesus' name, we pray. Amen.

Self-giving
Priorities
General

Loving God, these gifts represent portions of our earnings, hints of our best intentions, signs of developing generosity and growing faith. Put them to wholesome, healing, and holy use. We pray in the name of Jesus Christ. Amen.

Faith, development of
Generosity
Healing

O God, though beliefs are by nature unseen, we express ourselves as believers through visible acts of faithfulness. Help us, we pray, to do all that we do out of a commitment to follow Christ. And receive our gifts as affirmations of the faith we share. In Jesus' name. Amen.

Faithful living
Commitment
Affirmation

Loving God, as commitment to you provides a foundation for the living of our days, may these gifts we offer serve to support the mission of our church. By your grace, let our faithfulness grow upon the groundwork of joyful obedience and compassionate outreach. In Jesus' name we pray. Amen.

Obedience
Mission/service
Faith, foundation of

O God, we have gained earnings through the employment of our skills. Now we pray that you employ our earnings to strengthen the church in its work throughout the world. We ask this in Jesus' name. Amen.

Church
Work
General

O God, may the passing of these plates from hand to hand connect us in caring. And may the honesty of coming face to face with the needs of our church in the world guide us toward a gracious giving. We dedicate our offering and our continuing service to the Christ in whose name we pray. Amen.

Caring
Hands
World

O God, as the church is warmed by your love and leavened by the offerings in these plates, may it rise to new levels of hopefulness and service. And may these offerings also be a power of fermentation within the church, enabling us to quench the world's thirst with a new wine of compassion and peace. We pray in the name of Jesus Christ. Amen.

Peace
Communion
Mission/service

O God, we cannot calculate the measure of your grace, we cannot put a name to the extent of your love, we cannot picture the full majesty of your power. And yet we can respond to you, for our gifts express a thoroughgoing gratitude born of the Spirit that moves in our midst. Draw from us our best that we might offer it to you. In the name of Jesus Christ. Amen.

Gratitude
Priorities
Grace

O God, use the currency we offer in these plates to remind us that love is the currency of faith, for both have worth only when spent. Teach us to spend wisely in ways that show forth what we value. Receive our gifts and our giving, and may they be acceptable in your sight. In the name of Jesus Christ. Amen.

Self-giving
Values
Faithful living

Loving God, you have invested yourself in humanity through the presence of your Child, the provision of your Word, and the promise of your Spirit's action among us. May our offering of gifts and our commitment to faithful service be as dividends of grace. With grateful praise, we respond to your love through our giving. In Jesus' name. Amen.

Reformation Sunday
Grace
God, love of

O God, you provide what we cannot purchase or possess, unlimited resources of forgiveness and freedom. These are your gifts of love to us, and it is through their wise use that our faith finds expression. As people forgiven and free, as people afforded an opportunity to serve, we respond with these offerings and with an abiding thanks. In the name of Jesus Christ. Amen.

Stewardship
Forgiveness
Gratitude

O God, these plates contain but a portion of our thanks-giving. The remainder we offer through deeds of loving kindness, through service in the name of Christ, through enactment of the hope born of faithfulness. To the grace of your goodness we respond with gratitude, now and always, in the name of Jesus Christ. Amen.

Thanksgiving
Faithful living
God, responsiveness to

INTRODUCTIONS TO SILENT PRAYER

INTRODUCTIONS TO SILENT PRAYER

TWO FRIENDS who had both weathered some trying times met at a park one evening. This long-anticipated reunion took place after they had been apart for almost three years. They embraced, smiled, exchanged good-to-see-you pleasantries, and then began talking. They proceeded to speak at the same time or in alternating bursts of data-sharing. They were trying to catch up through hurried flurries of words. Both felt uneasy, and finally one of the friends suggested, "Let's try silence. Let's just be together for a while." So they sat down on a park bench surrounded by the sounds of the city. And over the next several minutes of shared interpersonal quiet, a recognition of their presence with one another replaced the absence that had separated them. The clutter of words had actually impeded reconnection and communication. Silence created a context for the growth of deep rapport.

We are an output-oriented society. We tend to measure value by productivity. We experience discomfort in silence, for it is not something we can control or direct toward predictable results. So we speak of silences that are "awkward," "deadly," or "oppressive." However, with regard to prayer, our silence serves us as it served the two friends. It helps us appreciate the presence of the One we are with, and it reminds us that our communication with God is not dependent on quantity of verbal output or quality of linguistic production. Silence before God, engaging us in the difficult discipline of listening, merits being labeled "grace-filled," "pregnant," or "liberating." As an exercise in attentiveness and intimacy, silent prayer may qualify as the ultimate in low-tech communication. It is not productive in a measurable sense, but it can provide us with the means of establishing a profoundly satisfying spiritual connection.

Following is a brief observation about a visual equivalent to silence. In drawing, sketching the outline of persons or objects is the most common technique used to create a simple representation on paper. But another option is taking notice of "negative space," then defining with lines the emptiness that frames the subject. When this is done, the figure or form seems to emerge out of a void. In a similar way, God emerges as a real and positive presence from the "negative space" of silent prayer. Artists use both techniques to create complete pictures. We can use both sound and silence to commune with God.

A certain church held a Christmas pageant every year, and the highlight of this pageant was a procession of the very youngest church-school children up to the Christ-child, before whom they deposited gifts wrapped in white tissue paper. Mary and Joseph were cued to nod to each child and to smile grateful, serene smiles. The procedure always went off without a hitch . . . except for the year when a certain little fellow changed things around a bit. He trundled up and deposited his gift as prescribed, but then, to the horror of the holy family, he picked up one of the baby Jesus' other packages and walked off with it. As the pint-sized kleptomaniac wandered back into the audience, his parents folded themselves into their folding chairs.

But the parents need not have shrunk in embarrassment. What their child had done pointed out something signified by the birth of Christ: in that birth, God told us that the new relationship with humanity was to be one of give-and-take, offering and receiving. The Christ-child receives gifts from children and other wise people. The Christ-child is a gift given to all.

Perhaps in silent prayer we can approach God with the unaffected innocence of that child at the pageant. We can reflect upon the ways we might offer the gifts of ourselves more completely. We can reflect upon the miraculous gifts we receive from God.

Advent
Christmas 🔲
Gifts

One of the pleasures of reading is its silence—yet what an active silence it is, for in it our minds and hearts are affected by materials we survey, and an unseen author enters our lives to speak to us through words on a page. Prayer has a similar level of activity, for *in* it we exercise our spirits, and *through* it we have contact with the Author of all creation. In silent prayer, we come now before God. [*Allow time for silent prayer.*]

> Hear our prayer, O God.
> To the weak-hearted, grant courage,
> In the brave-hearted, expand mercifulness,
> To the open-hearted, give focus,
> In the close-hearted, kindle kindness,
> To the light-hearted, offer service,
> In the heavy-hearted, create peace.
> We pray in the name of Jesus Christ. Amen.

God, as Author
Reading
Faith, heartfelt

Early in the nineteenth century, a group of English clergy were discussing the speaking abilities of some of their colleagues. Someone mentioned a particular archbishop who seemed unusually gifted with oratorical powers. The Rev. Sydney Smith, one of the group members, commented that he could indeed admire some of the things in the archbishop's discourses and noted especially a recent sermon. "In that address," said Smith, "he had some splendid flashes of silence." In the midst of our noisy, often hectic lives, we *need* some splendid flashes of silence to rest, to recoup, to settle our spirits, to commune with God in prayer. Let us pray in silence.

[*Allow time for silent prayer.*]

Speaking
Peace
Pause

A child built a tree house among the eight birch trees that grew in the backyard. The architecture looked like something from Frank Lloyd Wrong, but it was a special place to the child, a haven of quiet and aloneness. It was an imagining-place that became, at various times, a castle or a boat or a plane or a home of the future. And sometimes—not often, but sometimes—when the young builder sat looking silently through the trees at the neighborhood, seeing but unseen, the child wondered how God looked upon the creation. And in those times the child felt close enough to talk with God in questions. "Are you watching? How do things look to you, God? Are you glad you made us? Do you have fun?" With childlike questions formed within a tree-house silence, we can enter into prayer.

Faith, childlike
Curiosity, spiritual
Communion

One of the wonderful things about snow is that it tells silent stories—

• As it banks against a building or drifts in a field, it reveals the direction, strength, and course of the wind.
• As it receives the imprints of squirrel feet and dog paws, sled runners and boot bottoms, it records who has passed by.
• As it clings fresh-fallen to receptive evergreens, it announces its own weight to any who read the laden branches as scales.

When our prayers are silent as snow, they tell the story of God's receptiveness and presence. These prayers can be rich with meanings unheard in our noisier moments.

God, presence of
Seasons (winter)
Wind

The plants around us sink their roots into the ground for nourishment and support. They reach with stalks and trunks, branches and leaves, toward the light that gives them energy. In some ways, we are like these plants. We ground our lives in the events of the everyday, where nourishment comes from our work and play, support from the caring of family and friends. And we extend our spirits by stretching toward the light of God for the energy to grow, to become all we can be. We are both earth-bound and heaven-bound. Consider in silent prayer your rootings and your reachings, and thank God for the potential of miraculous growth.

Growth
Creation
Common things

In early elementary school, a portion of each day (usually right after lunch and recess) was set aside for something called "rest period." All of us would put our heads upon arms folded across our desks, and we would quietly rest. Many of us thought "rest period" was a stupid idea, too much like the hated naps we had left home to escape. But deep inside, we appreciated it. It was a silent, renewing, creative time that made the remainder of the day bearable . . . or at least better. In our silent prayer, we share a "rest period" with God. With heads bowed and hands clasped, we seek empowerment and refreshment.

Rest
Empowerment
Renewal

It is not difficult to figure out why silence often discomforts us. Certain phrases give silence a poor reputation.

"Shut up!"

"Button your lips!"

"Be still!"

"Keep quiet!"

These phrases are regularly delivered in a tone that suggests punishment. But there is nothing bad about silence.
It is a good and beautiful state. It exists as a playground of freedom, a building site for renewal, a sanctuary for our spirits.

So shut up, button your lips, be still, and keep quiet—
and enjoy God's gift of silence in the soundless conversation
of prayer.

Renewal

Freedom

Sanctuary

A good deal of excitement marks the beginning of every new baseball season. We are drawn to the game in part because of the moments of drama it offers to fans, moments when a hush falls over the crowd as pitcher and batter face one another in a decisive situation. We ardently wish for our own hero's success in the confrontation—the inning-ending strikeout or the screaming home run. If our hero triumphs, cheers pour forth. If our hero fails, we are prone to boo. Fans are notoriously fickle.

Jesus' entrance into Jerusalem marked the beginning of a new and apparently triumphant season of ministry. Yet within a matter of days, at just the decisive moment, the crowds hushed their cheers and turned upon their hero with catcalls and jeers. We, too, stand among that crowd as persons of fickle faith.

Silent prayer allows us to withdraw from the persuasive noises of the crowd. Within our silent prayer, we do well to ask God for courage to acknowledge our hero and Savior with increasingly steadfast love.

Palm Sunday
▩   Faith, fickle
Courage

When a butterfly emerges from the cocoon, its struggle is strenuous yet silent. The butterfly pauses after the ordeal, clinging limply to a branch before giving wing to its beautiful and newfound freedom.

Sometimes we bind ourselves into cocoons in a caterpillar-like way, confining and restricting ourselves, hiding ourselves away. But God transforms homely cocoon-dwellers into free and beautiful creatures. The power is miraculous and works upon us through time.

Whatever stage of development we are in—whether waiting within the cocoon or gathering our strength to fly or exulting in our flight—we can speak our silent prayers offering thanks and praise to God who transforms us and gives us freedom.

Easter
▩   Faith, development of
Transformation

Consider for a few moments the word "milieu." "Milieu" is a word no one seems comfortable pronouncing because it doesn't appear to be pronounced the way it is spelled. Somehow, no matter who says it, it comes out sounding as though that person were trying desperately to say "mildew" while sucking on a lemon. "Milieu" is a funny little word, but it is also a huge word full of meaning. Milieu is "environment," "setting," "context," and "happening" all wrapped up together.

Prayer, versatile instrument that it is, has countless milieus. But perhaps the best is a full and reverent silence.

Prayer, environment of
Pause
General

Perhaps we can best appreciate the wind on a completely calm day when nothing rustles or murmurs. Yet sometimes when we look up, we see clouds silently crossing the sky, subtly changing shapes and patterns. We wonder why the wind is distant. But if we are alert, we realize that even that faraway wind touches us as it moves clouds to make new pictures for our eyes. God, too, seems distant and unaffecting at times. Maybe we need the calm of silent prayer to realize that God's Spirit touches us always.

Spirit
Wind
Clouds

One of the skills most lacking in our culture is the skill of listening. Often, we scarcely hear what people have to say to us. We are too busy with other matters to give our attention to a person's words, or we have our own agenda to push or sales pitch to make, or we are listening only for what we want to hear and so miss what someone else needs to say. It has been noted that genuine communication is becoming a lost art, and that is largely because our skill as listeners has declined. So cries for help go unheeded, points of humor go unappreciated, words of love go unmarked, warnings go unheard. It is time to begin listening again, to declare our care by being receptive to others. And there is no better way to start than by pausing in prayer to listen to the God who speaks even through silence.

Listening
Pause
General

A friend of mine spent most Sunday afternoons of his childhood playing checkers with his grandfather. These matches were usually accompanied by baseball games on TV, and they were always halted for a vanilla pudding break. As the years passed, the boards enlarged to accommodate Grandpa's diminishing eyesight. Eventually, the checkers were the size of hockey pucks. This checkers time was a quiet time, with little said during a game other than the obligatory "King me." It was a communion time.

My friend tells me that he learned a great deal over the years of quiet Sundays as he lost every game he ever played with his grandfather. His grandfather, it seems, was something of a checkers genius, and from sitting at that table with him, my friend learned much about humility, patience, and respect for the ability that comes with practice and age. In all his losing, he was a winner because of what he learned.

Our quiet times of prayer with God are times of learning, too, times when we can commune and when we can mature in faith.

Faith, development of
Communion
Family

Home is a treasured place. Late at night, it can be a silent place, an environment for reading or thinking or praying or unwinding. Yet the silence is far from absolute, for when I listen to it, there are sounds that speak within it—the call of the whip-poorwill or killdeer, the hum of highway traffic, the popping of moths and beetles against a window screen—[*Choose noises to fit your locale*]. These are the usual components of quiet, the elemental sounds of silence. They are always there, and without them the silence would be dead. All I need to do to hear them is tune in.

I suggest that in silent prayer there is much to tune in: the cries of voiceless people, the soundless groans of a beleaguered earth, the tumblings around of our innermost thoughts and feelings, and the still, small voice of God.

Home
Listening
Justice

Consider for a moment how the God we gather to worship is like the horizon line between earth and sky—constantly present yet changing in form, ever visible yet not within our grasp, the point of contact at which this world meets all that is beyond.

Sometimes when the fog rolls in or the smog enshrouds or the clouds block off the distance, the horizon line moves closer. So it is that when we find ourselves in a spiritual fog or experience the smog of unclear choices or sense a cloud of sorrows about us, God draws nearer too.

Sometimes when the day is crisp, the air clean, the sun alive, the horizon line is sharp as a shadow upon a newly painted wall. And so it is that when we perceive the bright goodness of life or feel ourselves illumined in spirit, God seems clear and sharply defined.

By our presence as worshipers in this place, we affirm the importance of stretching ourselves toward the horizon of faithfulness where the mystical and the ordinary meet and merge, where the God out there becomes as well the God within.

Consider these things as we pray in silence.

Creation
God, reaching toward
Faith, experience of

BENEDICTIONS

BENEDICTIONS

GIVEN ITS DERIVATION from Latin (*bene* meaning "good," and *dictio* meaning "speech"), the word "benediction" has clear meaning. It can be defined simply as "good speech." In the context of worship, however, a benediction is a particular kind of good speech. Specifically, it is the brief blessing offered at the close of a service, or it is a form of service created to permit the setting-aside of certain items for sacred use. As the blessing issued prior to the dispersal of gathered worshipers, a benediction usually has a positive and reassuring tone. It may also challenge people not to leave the good news behind but to carry it into all the world. As a service of designating items to be used for holy purposes, a benediction may remind us of God's broader call to use our talents, our material goods, our very lives, in faith-expressive ways.

How do we customarily take leave of one another? We often do so automatically, as if we were clicking off a computer mouse or a television remote control. We often do so thoughtlessly, as if a mumbled "g'night" or a hasty "see ya" were the best we have to offer. Seldom are our words benedictions. In listening to or writing out benedictions for liturgical use, we have the opportunity to reflect upon our everyday words of departure. We have occasion to consider how to transform our common language into the living language of faith. What a beneficial change it would be if we broke contact with one another using genuinely good speech, the kind of speech that conveys heartfelt well-wishing, that affirms time apart as a sacred space filled with holy possibilities. God does watch between us while we are absent from one another (Gen. 31:49). That is the basis for every benediction.

Bear witness to God with us!
Cradle the creation and guard it from harm.
Love this life and handle it as a fragile gift.
Practice peace and work for the justice that sustains it.
Serve God well. Amen.

Advent
Creation
Justice

In the presence of God lies the promise of peace.
Pray for the triumph of justice and work for the wholeness
of humanity.
Be guided by faith in all you do.
And greet Emmanuel, the Christ and the Bringer of Peace,
with open, joyful hearts. Amen.

Advent
Peace
Justice

The stable abounds with animal sounds.
The sky is an empty stage.
But watch and wait,
For the manger will sigh with a newborn's cry
And a host will proclaim a new age. Peace be
with us. Amen.

Advent
Waiting
Hope

Allow your longings to speak from within.
Permit God's promise to occupy your minds and inhabit
  your hearts.
Prepare your spirits for the coming of Christ. Amen.

Advent
Preparation
Hope

Discover God's greatness in small beginnings,
God's grandeur in humble places,
God's glory in loving service.
Receive the coming joy, and magnify God in all
  you do. Amen.

Advent
Common things
Joy

Prepare to receive the coming of the Light.
Discover in the silence a carol's sounds.
A child comes to us this night,
And the love of God abounds.
Christ the Savior is born! Amen.

Christmas Eve
God, love of
Light

Glad tidings to you this Christmas day!
Exult in the child's birth.
Wonder at the depth of God's love.
And rejoice in a simple majesty that is God's way to be
   with us.
Grace, mercy, and peace dwell among us always. Amen.

Christmas
God, presence of
Joy

Go gently into the world—
with arms that embrace,
with minds that cut through untruth,
with hearts that capture enemies by strength of love.
Inheritors of the Spirit, brothers and sisters in Christ, peace
   be with you. Amen.

Christmastide
Faithful living
Peace

Keep faith as a quest.
Move with the Spirit,
And you will find a love redemptive and sustaining. Amen.

Epiphany
Faith, journey of
God, love of

Let us go now, as a people united in Christ, to reconcile what is divided, to heal what is broken, to bring together what is torn apart. By the power and grace of God, we are called to minister to one another in the name of the One who came for us all. Peace, joy, and love be among us in every new day. Amen.

Unity
Reconciliation
Healing

Let us go now in friendship with one another to sense the Spirit and to worship God in all we do. May we be inspired to live the way of Christ—to be healers, lovers, teachers, and friends to a world that is God's good creation. Amen.

Faithful living
Discipleship
Brotherhood/Sisterhood

Bear into the world, in the name of Christ, a cup of blessing and communion.

And feed, as the Spirit equips you, those who hunger for love and compassion, justice and peace.

May God watch between us while we are apart from one another. Amen.

Communion
Hunger
Mission/service

As apprentices of the servant Christ,
learn the essential skills of faith—
devoted prayer and determined action,
persistent hope and practiced love.
May your deeds reflect the wondrous grace
   of God. Amen.

Education
Faith, essentials of ▨
Mission/service

Reflect and repent, pray and proclaim.
Establish your footing on the love of God,
And let your faith be upstanding and firm. Amen.

Faith, essentials of
God, love of ▨
General

Cherish the creation and worship its Maker.
Establish peace and serve its Savior.
Honor the earth and seek its well-being.
Love your God in all you do. Amen.

Earth Day
God, as Creator ▨
Environment

Enact your faith in the exercise of love.
Make peace and do justice in honor of the Creator.
Offer comfort and extend consolation in the name
of Christ.
Savor time and enjoy life in partnership with the
Spirit. Amen.

One Great Hour of Sharing
World
Faithful living

May the peace of Christ inhabit our hearts and be at home in
our homes.
May it lead us to construct a just and wholesome future
hospitable to every child of today. Amen.

Peace
Home
Future

Lean upon God to be strong. Learn from God to be wise.
Seek out Christ to be found. Serve with Christ to be free.
Trust in the Spirit to be healthy. Live by the Spirit to be
whole. Amen.

God, reliance upon
Trinity
General

Immerse yourselves in deeds of faithfulness,
And find in all you do as Christ's people
Refreshment and renewal,
Empowerment and peace. Amen.

Faithful living
Renewal
Empowerment

Keep the love of God at the heart of your faith,
Let the pulse of the Spirit be felt through your deeds.
Serve in Christ's name with passion and power. Amen.

Palm Sunday
Faith, essentials of
Mission/service

Christ our Savior enters into hearts as into cities, with
  gentleness, joy, and grace.
We invite the presence, dare the discipleship, and feel the
  power of our Redeemer.
May the love and peace of Christ become ascendant in our
  lives. Amen.

Palm Sunday
Discipleship
Faith, heartfelt

In turning toward God, we face forward in faith.
Keep steadfast in devotion,
Devoted in prayer,
Prayerful in service.
May peace fill your spirits. Amen.

Maundy Thursday
Devotion
Faith, journey of

Beyond empty tombs and empty spirits,
There is abundant life and plentiful hope.
Live the joy of this day always. Christ is risen!
Alleluia and Amen.

Easter (Sunrise)
Joy
Faith, journey of

Spread the good news! Live for Christ because Christ lives in you! Let each new dawn bring a day of resurrection, for Christ is risen indeed. Alleluia and Amen.

Easter
Good news
Renewal

May God grant spiritual muscle to your commitment,
movement to your faith,
and gentleness to your deeds.
In a risen Redeemer, find new power and
    new life. Amen.

Eastertide
Commitment
Faith, strength of

Live a bold Easter faith that claims resurrection as
a reason for the affirmation of hope,
a resource for the restoration of wholeness,
a power for the fulfillment of promise. Amen.

Eastertide
Courage
God, power of

Trust in the Maker of all creation,
Honor God with an enormous faith,
And extend yourselves in love,
    for no one lives beyond the Spirit's reach.
Peace be with us. Amen.

God, trust in
Faithful living
General

By word and deed,
Through love offered and forgiveness accepted,
With sincere thanks and dedicated service,
Honor God, confess Christ, and live with Spirit. Amen.

Faithful living

Discipleship

General

Let go the fears that hinder trust,
the hesitancies that stifle hope,
the denials that block forgiveness.
Open yourself to grace and growth.
Let God form faith within you. Amen.

Grace

Fear

Faith, development of

In common life and ordinary time,
sense your Creator's presence,
serve Christ with extraordinary care,
and pay uncommon attention to the Spirit's guiding
    power. Amen.

Common things

Faith, attentiveness to

General

Hold firmly to faith by releasing it through your deeds—
derive love from God,
compassion from Christ,
empowerment from the Spirit.
And find contentment in worship and
    service. Amen.

Faith, sources of
Discipleship   ▧
Trinity

When the Holy Spirit breathes through us,
And the heartbeat of hope pulses within,
The vital signs of faith are strong.
    Live full well. And serve for the love of God. Amen.

Pentecost
Faith, heartfelt   ▧
Hope

Care for the earth and keep it well.
Preserve its life, cherish its beauty, respect its limits.
Regard it a holy habitation, the common home for all God's
    children. Amen.

Environment
Home   ▧
Faith, family of

Through all the turnings of time,
Let our actions revolve around the central presence
  of Christ,
And let them convey an ongoing return of praise to God.
May peace dwell in our midst and commitment to justice
  bond us together. Amen.

Time
Praise
Justice

Inform your faith by Word and Spirit.
Transform the world by practicing the peace of Christ.
Go forth as disciples,
So that through your believing in God you will be loving
  of others. Amen.

Discipleship
Transformation
Brotherhood/Sisterhood

Enact your faith with energy and intention.
As you open your lives to others,
May they read in your deeds the story of God's love and
  power. Amen.

Faith, story of
Faithful living
General

Live in God's presence,
Exult in life's promise,
Claim the gifts that are yours each day.
Serve gladly, knowing you have much to offer,
And so find the joy of Christ. Amen.

Joy
Mission/service
God, presence of

The week ahead is God's holy time. Cherish every moment as a gift of grace. Enjoy daily servings of work and play, communion and faith. Live in partnership with our loving God. Amen.

Time
Future
Joy

The God we worship at the common table and the high
   altar is one God.
So devour each new day with hearty appetite and glad
   thanksgiving, for there is a spiritual flavor in every
   second, a taste of the holy in every hour.
Live a full-course faith. Peace be within and among us.
   Amen.

Communion
Time
Faith, appetite for

Decide daily to be Christ's disciples.
Be free with faithfulness,
Lavish with love,
And selfless with service,
For each person you meet is a child of God.
Peace be with us and among us. Amen.

Choice
Faith, inclusiveness of
God, love of

May the love of God, shown in Christ, be known among us.
Uplift the weary, embrace the rejected, empower the
  oppressed, and so uphold the faith through deeds of
  compassion and grace. Amen.

World Communion Sunday
Mission/service
Faithful living

Develop your discipleship
Through solitary study and prayer,
Through corporate worship and witness.
Live the love of God. Amen.

Discipleship
Education
General

The challenge in change is holding true to faith.
May God's Spirit empower us and lead us in the way of
  the One upon whom our faith is founded.
Grace, mercy, and peace be in our midst. Amen.

Reformation Sunday
Change
Faith, steadfast

Invest yourselves in faith.
Value all persons as valuable in the sight of God.
Learn the worth of spiritual wealth,
And supply the needs of others as you accept the
  gifts of grace.
Peace be our way in the world. Amen.

Stewardship
Faith, as investment
Grace

Each day as we harvest the gifts of God's grace,
May our thanks be abundant, appreciative, and full.
With growing gratitude, serve well in
  Christ's name. Amen.

Thanksgiving
Grace
General

INDEX